Many couples, thinking they know each other intimately, have actually lived on a superficial level for years . . .

Although your husband is similar to other men, he is totally unique, one of a kind. He is different in temperament, personality, childhood, adolescence, family relationships, heritage, talents, goals, aspirations, successes, failures, frustrations and disappointments. You must abandon the idea that he's just like all other men, another common, everyday, average guy. Finding out who he is and what he feels can be one of the most challenging, stimulating and rewarding experiences of your life.

FOR BETTER OR FOR BEST

BY GARY SMALLEY
with Steve Scott

HarperPaperbacks
A Division of HarperCollinsPublishers

The stories in this book are true.
The names have been changed
except for references to the author.

HarperPaperbacks   *A Division of* HarperCollins*Publishers*
                    10 East 53rd Street, New York, N.Y. 10022

This book is published by arrangement with Zondervan
Publishing House.

Unless otherwise indicated, Scripture is from the New
American Standard Bible © 1960, 1962, 1963, 1968, 1971,
1972 by the Lockman Foundation.

First HarperPaperbacks printing: March 1991

Printed in the United States of America

HarperPaperbacks and colophon are trademarks of
HarperCollins*Publishers*

10 9 8 7 6 5 4 3 2 1

To my wife,
Norma,
who made my contribution to this book possible,
and to our children
Kari, Greg, and Michael

Special Thanks

For those who helped with the first edition.

Bonney Scott:
> For her loving commitment which made the scheduled completion of this book possible.

Robert J. Marsh:
> For his vision and encouragement, without which this book would not have been written for at least three years.

The Principals of R.M. Marketing:
> For their courage in committing the financial resources that made our dream a reality.

Harry Howard:
> For coordinating the layout and physical production of this book.

The Editorial Staff:
> Judy Baggett Thrasher and Linda Allen Fyke for enabling us to complete a two-year project in two months.

The Typists:

Anna Ruth Hart, Betty Snyder, Lisa Bland, Darlene Williams, Janet Perry, and Denise Duck for working their fingers to the bone.

Contents

Almost Too Late

I always thought I was a pretty good husband. When I first approached Gary about writing a book together, I had no idea what I was getting myself into. As I worked on his material, I became painfully aware of what my wife has had to put up with for the past ten years. Chapter after chapter inflicted a deep conviction of the countless ways I had failed as a husband to love my wife. At times I could not even work on the book because it exposed my shortcomings as a husband and father.

I can honestly say that the content of this book has helped give me an overwhelming desire to honor and love my wife as the precious and unique person she is. I trust it will give you the insights and encouragement you need to enter into the reality of a fulfilling relationship with your husband.

Steve Scott

Introduction

Fulfilling marriages don't just happen. They are built on proven principles essential to the development of any warm and loving relationship. Part 1 (chapters 1 through 6) is designed to help you better understand these principles and to learn how you can apply them in a practical way to your everyday routine. These principles are the foundation of a good marriage.

Part 2 (chapters 7 through 16) provides the materials you need to build on this foundation. Each chapter cites specific ways to motivate your husband to love you genuinely, in the way you want to be loved. Each chapter is written independently of the others, so you can read them in any order you wish. Their order of appearance is based on priorities women have said are the most important to them. However, your unique situation may mean that a later chapter will be more vital to you than an earlier one. To determine what chapters are of greatest importance to you, number the ten summary statements below according to their relative importance to you. You may then want to read the chapters in your own order of importance.

- ☐ 7. How to increase your husband's desire to spend more time with you.
- ☐ 8. How to increase your husband's eagerness to listen to you with undivided attention on a consistent basis.
- ☐ 9. How to increase your husband's sensitivity to your emotional and romantic needs and desires.
- ☐ 10. How to motivate your husband to comfort you when you're down.
- ☐ 11. How to motivate your husband to receive your correction without defensiveness.
- ☐ 12. How to inspire your husband to gain a sincere appreciation for you and learn to praise you.
- ☐ 13. How to encourage your husband to assume responsibility with the children and assist you with your household needs.
- ☐ 14. How to motivate your husband to meet your material needs with a cheerful attitude.
- ☐ 15. How to increase and deepen your husband's affection for you.
- ☐ 16. How to stimulate your husband's desire to be your most intimate friend.

PART I

1

Lasting Relationships Don't Just Happen

"An excellent wife, who can find? For her worth is far above jewels."

Proverbs 31:10

Jim stared silently at the television set while Carol ached inside, wondering why he was angry at her again. They had only been married a year, and Carol could already see their relationship deteriorating. She couldn't help but wonder if she would soon join the millions of other couples whose marriages have ended in divorce. When she finally broke the silence by asking Jim what was wrong, he refused to answer her. Hurting for a few minutes, she repeated the question. His response wounded her so deeply she began to doubt her adequacy as a wife.

He said, "I'm sick and tired of you taking everything so seriously. You're just too sensitive! If I had known you were this emotional, I probably never would have married you. But since we are married, I think you need to do your part. Cut out the overreacting and stop being so touchy about what I say and do. If we're going to have any kind of marriage, you have to stop being so childish!"

FOR BETTER

Sound familiar? With these harsh words, Jim unknowingly has set their relationship on a destructive path leading to some very unattractive changes—changes, which will likely lead to the ultimate disintegration of their relationship. Jim's main problem, shared by thousands of other husbands, is that he fails to understand the basic difference between the natures of men and women. Jim has taken two of his wife's greatest natural strengths, her sensitivity and intuitive awareness of life, and labeled them weaknesses. In response to Jim's reproof, Carol, like thousands of other wives, will begin to form a calloused, hardened attitude toward life in general and Jim in particular. If their marriage lasts more than a few years, Jim will find to his dismay that Carol's sensitivity has finally been subdued and that he has lost most or all of his attraction to her. If only he could remember that her sensitivity was one of the first things that attracted him. If only he understood that her alertness was one of her greatest strengths, and if he began treating her with tenderness, gentleness, and kindness, their relationship would grow stronger and more fulfilling.

The emotional and mental differences between men and women (described in detail in chapter 3) *can* become insurmountable obstacles to a lasting, fulfilling relationship when ignored or misunderstood. However, those same differences, when recognized and appreciated, can become stepping-stones to a meaningful, fulfilling relationship.

Women, for example, have a tremendous advantage in two of life's most important areas: loving God and loving others (Matt. 22:36–40). Women have an intuitive ability to develop meaningful relationships and a desire for intimate communication, and this gives them the edge in what Jesus described as the two greatest commandments. Loving God and others is building relationships. God said that it was not good for man to dwell alone, and He created a significant Helper and Completer—woman. Men definitely need help with making and maintaining relationships, but *how* women help so that men listen and receive it is the thrust of this book.

When a woman understands her strengths for what they are, her self-image will be practically indestructible, no matter how her husband belittles her. When both husband and wife understand each other and begin to respond to one another accordingly, their relationship can blossom into the marriage they dreamed of. Carol can begin to make Jim aware of her deeper needs for love, assurance, and security, without feeling selfish for desiring fulfillment of her needs. Unfortunately, at the rate Jim and Carol are going, it probably won't be long before they join the ranks of the one-million-plus couples divorced each year in the United States.

But don't despair! *Your* marriage does *not* have to become part of these awesome statistics. With the right tools, you *can* carve a more fulfilling marriage out of a seemingly hopeless one, and this book will provide you with many of those tools. But the tools by themselves will never get the job done. They have to be picked up and used *properly* and *consistently* if they are to bring the intended results.

If your husband is willing to work beside you, you'll strengthen your marriage that much faster. That's why I believe the greatest benefits will result when this book is used in conjunction with the book for your husband, *If Only He Knew*. When a husband understands his wife's needs and learns how to meet those needs, the relationship will grow more quickly.

In counseling, I have found that *if* I can get the husband to do his part *first*, it's much easier for the wife to carry out her responsibilities in the relationship with greater enthusiasm and commitment. Unfortunately, women are usually more concerned about deepening their marital relationships than men. That's why your book was written first; I felt that *you* would be the one with the greater interest in strengthening your marriage and the one to initiate change in the relationship.

I also believe that you will be the *key* to motivate your husband to read his book. Consequently, a whole chapter in this book (chapter 5) explains how to motivate your husband to read his corresponding book, *If Only He Knew*. If he reads his book carefully, I feel confident that he will *begin* to become aware of the special person you really are and will begin treating you with more tenderness, gentleness, sensitivity, and understanding.

If your relationship with your husband is less than you desire and he shows little concern for your feelings, you may at first find it difficult to take the steps given in this book. However, if you are willing to overlook his lack of response for the moment and put forth some extra effort, the ideas presented in this book *can work*. I am also confident that your husband's desire for a better relationship will increase in response to the *changes* he *sees* in you.

I have spoken to hundreds and hundreds of married women. I found very few who did not want an improvement in their relationships with their husbands. Some women were more content than others, but most of them longed for more loving and romantic husbands. Many said they wanted their husbands to love them more than he loved anyone or anything. You might think, "That's impossible. There's not a man alive who loves like that!" But I have personally seen a growing number of husbands transformed into "impossible" lovers. The changes necessary don't just happen though, men *make* them happen when they know *what* to do!

ONE BIG REASON MARRIAGES FAIL

All too often, people marry before acquiring the knowledge and skills necessary to take care of their mates: to meet their emotional, mental, and physical needs. One of the ironies in our society is that a person has to have four years of training to receive a plumber's license, but absolutely no training is required for a marriage license. Our educational system doesn't even require communication courses basic to the meaningful development of any relationship. As a result, many men and women enter marriage with virtually no knowledge of how to meet the *basic* emotional and mental needs of their mates. And I must confess, I was certainly among the untrained when I married. It has taken my wife, Norma, and my friends many years to help me become a more loving husband.

It is typical for a man to marry without knowing *how* to talk to his wife. Some men don't even know that their wives *need* intimate communication. Often a man is completely unaware of his wife's sensitive nature. He doesn't know that things he considers trivial can be extremely important to her—things like anniversaries and holidays. Nor does he realize why such things *are* special to her, and so he is unable to meet her needs. Many men don't understand a woman's physical cycles and the hormonal changes she experiences. They don't realize how a woman's home, children, family, and friends become an interwoven part of her identity.

Many women step into marriage equally handicapped. They don't understand that admiration is to a man what romance is to a woman. They don't realize that a man generally relies on reasoning rather than intuitive sensitivity.

It is obvious, then, that if both husband and wife lack the

vital knowledge and skills to meet each other's needs, their needs will go unmet. One of the great psychiatrists of our time, Dr. Karl Menninger, said that when our basic needs are not met, we move in one of two directions. We either withdraw in "flight" or turn to "fight." The woman who takes the "flight" approach is certainly not escaping her problems. As she runs, she begins to doubt her self-worth. On the other hand, if she takes the "fight" approach, she may become an unattractive nag to her husband.

I believe the ideal marriage evolves when the wife concentrates on meeting her husband's needs and the husband concentrates on meeting his wife's needs. That combination builds the lasting qualities of a giving relationship.

This book was written to show women how to motivate their husbands to improve their relationship. Changes don't happen overnight, but the principles, in this book have been proven over time in thousands of marriages. I know they work. If a woman is willing to spend the time and energy necessary to apply these principles, I am confident she will see her marriage become more of what she desires.

If you want to become a great painter, you must be dedicated. Learning to master the essential techniques and skills of painting comes first. Then, after you have painted hundreds of canvases, you might display your work as an inspiration for young artists to follow. In the same way, I believe this book will give you many of the essential techniques and skills fundamental to making your marriage, with time and effort, a living example for others to follow.

Since this book was written to meet the needs of thousands of people, some of the principles and ideas contained in it are, naturally, general and far-reaching. It cannot possibly answer all of the specific questions every woman would like to ask, but it does attempt to address the major aspects of love and marriage.

FOR PERSONAL REFLECTION

Why is a wife so important to her husband? (See Genesis 2:18; Matthew 22:36–40.)

2

Eight Ways Husbands Hurt Their Wives

*"And if he sins against you seven times a day, and returns to
you seven times, saying, 'I repent,' forgive him."*
Luke 17:4

On a flight from Philadelphia to New Orleans, I mentioned to one of the stewardesses that I was writing a book about marriage. I told her one of the chapters discussed ways that a man hurts a woman without even realizing it. Before I knew it, I had been whisked up to first class and three stewardesses were telling me all of the ways their ex-husbands had hurt them. The three seemed amazed that a man could understand how words and actions, which seemed so innocent to their husbands, had inflicted hurts they, as women, could never forget.

For most couples with whom I counsel, a week rarely passes without the husband saying or doing something that unintentionally offends the wife. The following true stories illustrate *eight* ways that husbands hurt their wives . . . without even knowing it! However, I have seen men *stop* inflicting these hurts when their wives began applying some of the appropriate principles discussed in detail later.

11

HE FREQUENTLY CRITICIZES YOU

Jim was great at finding all of Sarah's faults.

Sarah had just slipped into her swimsuit and couldn't wait to get down to the beach. It was the first day of their vacation. Jim walked in, pinched her on the side, and casually remarked, "We better watch how much we eat on this trip." It seemed innocent to Jim, but Sarah thought he was really saying, "You're fat and ugly." The hurt was so deep that even to this day, five years and a divorce later, Sarah is extremely self-conscious in a swimsuit. (Oddly enough, Sarah is an attractive woman with a good figure.)

Several weeks after Jim made this remark, Sarah decided to try to do something about her figure. She concluded that ice skating would give her the necessary exercise. When she told Jim about her decision, he sarcastically said, "What do you want to do, become an Olympic champ?" To her, he was really saying, "I can't believe how stupid you are to come up with such a ridiculous idea. You're not worth the money it would cost."

Jim not only called attention to her weight problem but also criticized her for wanting to improve. Although he didn't realize it, Jim could find fault with almost anything Sarah said or did. He thought he could motivate her to change through sarcastic comments. Since a woman is not hard and calloused by nature, hurtful criticism rarely provides motivation to change. It usually brings deeper despair, which results in a diminished desire to please her husband. Chapters 10 and 12 will show you *how* to motivate your husband to replace his criticisms with appreciation and gratefulness.

OR FOR BEST

HE DOESN'T PAY ATTENTION TO YOUR WORDS AND IDEAS

The only way Julia could hope to get Harry's undivided attention would be to magically transform herself into a TV program.

It was 11:00 at night, and Susan, half-asleep, answered the phone. Across the line came the sobs of her mother thousands of miles away.

"What's wrong, Mom?"

Her mother replied, "I have to take $450 out of savings and buy your father a new color TV."

Now fully awake, Susan asked, "What happened?"

"For weeks I have been trying to get your father's attention long enough to explain a sensitive problem your little sister has had. I couldn't drag your father away from the TV set long enough to tell him. Finally I couldn't take it any longer. I marched into the den with a hammer, stepped between him and the TV, and with one blow smashed the screen in!"

"Mom, it could have exploded and you could have been hurt."

"I know, but I really didn't care. I just wanted him to listen. You know what your father did?"

"What?"

"You're not going to believe it. He just got up, walked into the bedroom, locked the door, and turned the little TV on to the program he had been watching in the den. He didn't say a word. He just went right back to ignoring me."

This example may seem extreme, but many wives are understandably offended by their husbands' lack of attentiveness. When a wife begins to talk, it almost seems like a mechanism goes off inside the husband's brain that says, "Now's the time to pick up the newspaper, turn on the TV, or start trying to solve the latest problem at work." He may show his inattentiveness by focusing his eyes on something else (like the spot on the tablecloth) or by simply gazing with a blank expression into his wife's eyes while his mind retreats to other playgrounds.

BUT when it's his turn to talk, he not only demands her attention, but expects her to remember every detail, as if the entire conversation were permanently recorded in her mind.

A woman can be deeply hurt by her husband's inattentiveness because it indirectly tells her that he considers her concerns insignificant and unimportant.

Don't despair. Chapter 8 will teach you how to gain his consistent, undivided attention . . .AND IT WORKS.

HE DOESN'T ASSUME ENOUGH OF THE HOUSEHOLD RESPONSIBILITIES

Mike thought his only responsibility was to bring home the paycheck.

At 6:45 on Friday morning Mike was just beginning to wake up. As he heard the three children yelling at each other, he noticed that his wife, Betty, had left their bedroom door open. "Just once I wish I could sleep till seven," he muttered. Then he yelled, "As long as you're going to leave my door open, can't you at least keep the kids quiet so I can get some rest?"

He didn't stop to think that Betty had been up for an hour, fixing the children's lunches, getting them ready for school, and cooking breakfast at the same time. And he had the nerve to tell her she wasn't even doing that right because she had left his door open and disturbed his sleep. *Why doesn't he get up and help me? Do I need any less sleep than he does? Are the children my sole responsibility?*

If Mike had had the audacity to take it one step further that morning by asking Betty why she never made a hot breakfast for him, she probably would have told him, "If you want a hot breakfast, set your cornflakes on fire!"

Like a lot of men, Mike thinks his responsibility to his family ends when he leaves the office.

And so does Tom.

Jenny, a stewardess, came home half-dead after a grueling four days in the air. As usual, her "welcome-home" consisted of four days' worth of dirty dishes, four days' worth of unemptied ash trays, and four days' worth of mess scattered all over the house. As she walked into the family room, her husband kept watching the 6:00 news and greeted her by saying, "I'm really glad you're home. This place is beginning to look like a dump."

Don't feel you're the only woman with a husband who doesn't help out much around the house. Probably you don't even talk about it with him because he makes you feel like a nag. Quick to remind you how hard he works and how much pressure he bears, he may even make you feel like a failure because you can't do it adequately by yourself.

Chapter 13 should be just the good news you need to help your husband assume a fair share of the household responsibilities. And you won't have to nag at all.

YOUR NEEDS AND DESIRES ARE ALWAYS SECONDARY TO HIS ACTIVITIES

Fred was always too busy with something else when his wife needed him; but he always found time to watch TV, read the paper, or go out with the boys.

Fred was a wealthy architect who frequently told his wife he needed several days without her interruption to "think through" a design. However, he had no problem taking a break to watch TV, play a round of golf, or go to lunch with his friends.

In fact, even when he wasn't working on a project, he was usually busy doing things he wanted to do, rather than spending time with his wife. She finally *resigned* herself to the fact that she and her world were not important enough to compete for his attention and companionship.

There are at least six ways you can increase your husband's desire to consider your needs. These are discussed in chapter 7.

HE TRIES TO EXPLAIN YOUR HURTS INSTEAD OF JUST TRYING TO UNDERSTAND YOUR FEELINGS AND EMPATHIZE WITH YOU

When Sandy put a dent in Mark's new car, she needed his shoulder . . . not his mouth.

Sandy works hard to make a nice home for her husband and their children. One afternoon while pulling their car into the garage, she hit a post. Knowing he would be upset, she was already in tears by the time he came out of the house. Mark could have become her knight-in-shining-armor by putting his arm around her and simply saying, "That's okay, dear. I know how you feel. Forget the car. I'll take care of it. What can I do to make you feel better now?"

Instead, Mark ran up to the car, looked at the dent, looked up at Sandy, and said, "Where did you get your driver's license . . . Sears & Roebuck? Get out of the car and let me park it." Then he went on to tell her how elementary it is to avoid the posts and drive correctly into the garage.

Men are great lecturers on everything from losing weight to taking care of the house. But how can you get a man to step off the podium and learn how to give you his shoulder to lean on while he quietly and gently comforts you? In chapter 10, I reveal three steps you can take to teach and motivate your husband to comfort you in those tense times when he's tempted to lecture or ignore you.

HE ACTS AS IF HE'S SUPERIOR AND YOU'RE INFERIOR

Larry always acted as if he were smarter and his ideas were better than Joann's.

Larry and Joann both graduated from college with honors. His degree was in engineering, hers in home economics. Month after month, Larry said and did things that made Joann feel as if she added no significant intellectual worth to the marriage. He never took her advice, yet he was always quick to express his opinion, even when it related to her areas of expertise. From cooking to room decor, he could always tell her how to do it better. Also, he was usually making comparisons: his major to her major, the difficulty of his work versus the ease of hers, etc. He consistently demonstrated to her that he neither appreciated her qualities nor respected her talents. Essentially, he made her feel like a doormat.

God never created a woman to be a doormat. She is meant to be a vital, life-giving part of the home. Women have many rich, natural qualities not natural to men. Some of these qualities are detailed in the next chapter. Chapters 11 and

12 explain how your husband can gain a genuine respect and admiration for your uniqueness.

HE SHOWS PREFERENCE TO OTHERS OVER YOU

It seemed only natural for Brad to defend John; after all, John was his best friend.

Karen wasn't married to Brad for long before she learned that she should never express her lack of appreciation for any of Brad's friends or relatives. One day Brad came home from work and saw Karen popping a chicken into the oven. He was delighted because that meant he would have time to toss the football with John for a while. On the way out, he told Karen that he was going over to John's house. She replied, "I hate him. You always spend time with him when you come home instead of with me." Brad stopped dead in his tracks and came back in. He told her she should be ashamed of herself after all John had done for them. John's encouragement had kept them together during their courting days, and John's encouragement had helped them through their first difficult months of marriage. Now she was acting immature and childish, attacking the one who had been more like a brother than a friend.

When she started crying, Brad thought she understood the point he was making; he thought she was feeling ashamed. Not quite! His statement said to her loud and clear that he preferred John over her as a person and as a companion. As time went on, she learned by his words, actions, and attitudes that he preferred many people over her: relatives, business associates, friends, secretaries, even casual acquaintances.

Never did he defend her to anyone, and yet he always rose to everyone else's defense anytime she voiced a criticism.

You'll be happy to know that now, years later, Brad consistently prefers Karen above all others. Anytime there is a disagreement between her and anyone else (even his mother), he takes her side and tries to help the other person see the matter from Karen's point of view. In fact, some of his close friends can't understand why he has so much fun spending more recreation time with his wife than with them. In chapter 16 I discuss five practical things you can do that will inspire your husband to prefer you above all others.

HE DOESN'T GO OUT OF HIS WAY TO ADD ROMANCE TO YOUR RELATIONSHIP

Maryann still can't forget "the day" Frank forgot.

Frank was on a business trip, but Maryann knew she would soon be getting a call or a card or a telegram, or maybe even a bouquet of flowers from him, wishing her a happy birthday. When the mail came around noon, she ran to the box, but there was no card from Frank. She was disappointed at first but finally realized that he had probably decided on something more creative. After all, according to his associates, he was one of the most creative men in his company.

By 6:00 in the evening she ruled out flowers and a telegram because it was after business hours. *He must be planning a call,* she thought. She finally fell asleep around midnight— still nothing. The next day she was depressed but figured he would probably be bringing a surprise when he got home. When he came home, his hands were empty. He had completely forgotten about her birthday. She never said anything, but now, after sixteen years of marriage, she still hasn't forgotten. In fact, she confides that he doesn't do any of the romantic things he did when they were younger. Most of the romance, the unexpected "little things," are gone.

Isn't it amazing how some men who are so romantic before marriage can become so unromantic afterward? It almost seems like a piece of their brain was removed when they said "I do." They literally can't remember how to be romantic. When confronted directly, they are quick to question, "Well, what do you want me to do, buy you flowers or something?" As if there were one thing they could do to make everything right. Ironic isn't it . . . you probably didn't even have to give them a suggestion on romance before marriage, but now they need an entire education.

Other actions and comments can inflict hurt, causing deep depression and despair. Some of the deepest pain you feel comes from being criticized for simply responding to some of his negative qualities. For years I thought a very close friend was married to a "nag." Then I realized her nagging was partly a result of his irresponsibility and laziness in so many areas.

Another friend told me she wished she could explain to her husband that he has trained her to yell. It's the only way she can capture his undivided attention, fleeting as it is! I'm happy to say that she learned how to gain his undivided attention on a consistent basis in a way that has brought encouragement to both of them.

The goal of this book is to equip you with positive steps of action that will build and strengthen your relationship and fill it with genuine love that lasts. Don't think it's too late. I've seen too many marriages that were supposedly "lost causes" rebuilt beyond the wives' wildest expectations. And yours doesn't have to be the exception.

Before we can go any further, however, there are several

rarely discussed differences between men and women that must be understood in order to have a full appreciation for the principles we'll discuss later.

FOR PERSONAL REFLECTION

The biblical concept of forgiveness has *two* basic thrusts:
1. to release a person from the just guilt and consequences of his/her actions toward us, and
2. to release a person from the basic cause for his/her offensive behavior.

Have you considered the commitment of truly helping your husband learn how he offends you and also helping him become free from whatever causes him to be offensive?

Forgiveness is a lifelong process (Matt. 18:21,22). How many times do we forgive others?

3

The Hidden Reasons Men Act
The Way They Do

"And let the wife see to it that she respect her husband."
                                                              Ephesians 5:33

How can a man say something to his wife that cuts her to the core and an hour later expect her to respond romantically to his advances? Why does a man feel obligated to lecture his wife when he sees that her feelings are hurt? How can a man lie next to his crying wife, giving her the silent treatment, when she so desperately needs his compassion and concern?

These situations are not the exception; they are the norm in American marriages. When couples come to my office for help, they are usually surprised that I don't fall out of my chair in total shock as they tell me their feelings. They can't believe their experiences are common. Every marriage and every person is unique, yet the problems people experience are practically universal.

Many of the problems couples experience are based on one simple fact. Men and women are TOTALLY different. The differences—emotionally, mentally, and physically—are so extreme that if a husband and wife don't put forth a *concentrated effort* to gain a realistic understanding of each other, it is nearly impossible for them to have a happy marriage. A famous psychiatrist once said, "After thirty years of studying women, I ask myself, 'What is it that they really want?' " If this was his conclusion, imagine how little your husband really knows about you!

The purpose of this chapter is to help you understand some differences between you and your husband that are responsible for many of the problems within your relationship. This chapter should be encouraging to you because it will enable you to see *why* he does many of the things that hurt you. Chances are, you have always assumed he didn't care about the fact that he hurts you.

The fact is, he is a man, and many of the hurtful and calloused actions you have witnessed are simply the result of his basic nature as a man. This does not mean you have to resign to living with a calloused or insensitive man—quite the contrary. Once you understand some of the basic differences we will discuss, you will be able to help him balance his natural tendencies.

Before we look at precise physiological and psychological differences, let me first draw your attention to the general differences and how they affect your relationship. The best example I can think of to illustrate these differences is to compare the butterfly with the buffalo. The butterfly has a keen sensitivity. It is sensitive even to the slightest breeze. It flutters above the ground where it can get a panoramic awareness of its surroundings. It notices the beauty of even the tiniest of flowers. Because of its sensitivity, it is constantly aware of all of the changes going on around it and is able to react to the slightest variation in its environment. Thus, the butterfly reacts with swiftness toward anything that might hurt it. (Try to catch one without a net sometime.) If a tiny pebble were taped to its wing, the butterfly would be severely injured and eventually die.

The buffalo is another story. It is rough and calloused. It doesn't react to a breeze. It's not even affected by a thirty-mile-an-hour wind. It just goes right on doing whatever it was doing. It's not aware of the smallest of flowers, nor does it appear to be sensitive to slight changes in its environment. Tape a pebble to the buffalo's back and he probably won't even feel it.

The buffalo isn't "rotten to the core" just because he goes around stepping on pretty flowers. In fact, the buffalo's toughness is a tremendous asset. His strength, when harnessed, can pull a plow that four grown men can't pull.

The analogy should be obvious. Your husband is the buffalo (Don't say amen too loudly!) and you're the butterfly. He may tend to "plow" through circumstances, while you "feel" life and your surroundings with much more sensitivity. The "pebble on the butterfly's wing" may take the form of a sarcastic remark, a sharp criticism, or even an indifferent attitude. Whatever it is, it can hurt and even crush you, while he may not even notice what he's done.

The analogy ends in that the buffalo can never take on any of the butterfly's sensitivities, and the butterfly will never benefit from the buffalo's strength.

Such is not the case with your marriage. Your husband CAN learn how to be gentle, sensitive, and romantic, but he probably won't learn by himself; that's why I've written this book . . . to show you how you can help him. You must realize that your husband doesn't understand how much his cutting words or indifferent attitudes actually affect your feelings. He can learn, but you'll need to help him.

Now, let's take a look at some of the differences between

men and women. We will discuss mental, emotional, physical, sexual, and intuitive differences. Each section is by no means exhaustive but will at least give you a better understanding of the differences we tend to overlook.

MENTAL/EMOTIONAL DIFFERENCES

Women tend to be more "personal" than men. Women have a deeper interest in people and feelings, while men tend to be more preoccupied with practicalities that can be understood through logical deduction.

Dr. Cecil Osborne says that women tend to become "an intimate part" of the people they know and the things that surround them; they enter into a kind of "oneness" with their surroundings. A man relates to people and situations, but he usually doesn't allow his identity to become entwined with them. He somehow remains apart. That's why a woman, viewing her house as an extension of herself, can become easily hurt when it is criticized by others. (One woman in her midfifties said she enjoys a card or flowers from her husband because they separate her from her identity with her home and family. The gift singles her out as an individual, with an individual's identity and self-worth.)

Because of a woman's emotional identification with people and places around her, she needs more time to adjust to change than a man does. A man can logically deduce the benefits of a change and get "psyched up" for it in a matter of minutes. Not so with a woman. She focuses on the immediate consequences of the change and the difficulties it may involve for her and her family. She needs time to get over the initial adjustment before she can begin to warm up to the advantages of the change.

Steve and Bonney had been struggling to make just enough money to put food on the table. His small business was requiring eighteen hours a day on his part, and she was putting in at least eight hours a day (and was seven months pregnant). Steve flew East to show his business ideas to a multimillionaire. The man was impressed and made Steve a generous offer. Steve could hardly wait to call Bonney and tell her the great news.

It took Steve less than five minutes to accept the offer. It was the only "reasonable" course of action. He called Bonney and told her the news in "logical" order so she could get as excited as he was. He told her, "First, you won't have to work any more. Second, he's giving me 20 percent of the profits (He says I'll be a millionaire in a year.). Third, you won't believe how beautiful it is back here, and he's going to pay all the moving expenses."

Steve was shocked when Bonney began to weep uncontrollably. At first he thought she was crying for joy (I know it's hard to believe that he actually thought that, but remember, men can be like buffalos.).

As soon as Bonney caught a breath between sobs, she had a chance to ask some questions, which Steve considered totally ridiculous. (In fact, he thought her mind had snapped.) She asked questions like, "What about our parents?" and "What about our apartment—I just finished the room for the baby?" With her third question, Steve, with all of his masculine "sensitivity," abruptly terminated the phone call. She had the nerve to ask if he'd forgotten she was seven months pregnant!

After giving her an hour or two to pull herself together, he called her back. She had gained her composure and agreed to move East and leave her parents, her friends, her doctor and childbirth classes, and the nursery she had spent so much time preparing for her first child.

It took Bonney almost eight months to adjust to a change that Steve had adjusted to in minutes. Steve never made his million. The business failed eight days before their baby was born, and they moved again to another place, still 3,000 miles from home. Steve eventually learned his lesson, and today he doesn't make any major change unless Bonney is in total agreement. He tries to give her ample time to adjust to other changes as soon as he can foresee them. However, Steve will never forget the loving sacrifices his wife made so many times. He even realizes that questions like "What about our parents?" or "What about the nursery?" can be more meaningful than money.

PHYSICAL DIFFERENCES

According to Dr. Paul Popenoe, founder of the American Institute of Family Relations in Los Angeles, a book could be filled with the biological differences between the sexes, excluding those differences related to reproduction. Here are a few of these differences:

Men and women differ in every cell of their bodies. This difference in the chromosome combination is the basic cause of development into male or female as the case may be.

Women have greater constitutional vitality, perhaps because of this chromosome difference. Normally, they outlive men by four to eight years (in the U.S.).

Women's basal metabolism is normally lower than men's.

They differ in skeletal structure. Women have a shorter head, broader face, less protruding chin, shorter legs, and longer trunk.

There are also internal differences. Women have a larger stomach, kidneys, liver, and appendix, but smaller lungs than men.

In bodily functions, women have several important ones totally lacking in men—menstruation, pregnancy, lactation. Women's hormones are different and more numerous than men's. These hormonal differences influence behavior and feelings.

The thyroid gland behaves differently in the two sexes. Women's thyroid is larger and more active. Consequently, it enlarges during pregnancy and during menstruation; it makes her more prone to goiter, provides resistance to cold, is associated with the smooth skin, relatively hairless body, and thin layer of subcutaneous fat.

Women's blood contains more water than men's (20 percent fewer red cells). Since the red cells supply oxygen to the body cells, women tire more easily and are more prone to faint. Their constitutional viability is, therefore, strictly a long-range matter. When the working day in British factories was increased from ten to twelve hours under wartime conditions, accidents increased 150 percent among women, but not at all among men.

In brute strength, men are 50 percent above women.

Women's hearts beat more rapidly (80 beats per minute vs. 72 for men). Their blood pressure (10 points lower than men) varies from minute to minute, but they have much less tendency to have high blood pressure—at least until after menopause.

Women's breathing power is significantly lower than men's.

Women withstand high temperatures better than men because their metabolism slows down less.

SEXUAL DIFFERENCES

Women's sexual drive tends to be related to their menstrual cycles, while men's drive is fairly constant. The hormone testosterone is a major factor in stimulating men's sexual desire.

Women are stimulated more by touch and romantic words. They are far more attracted by a man's personality, while men are stimulated by sight. Men are usually less discriminating about those to whom they are physically attracted.

While a man needs little or no preparation for the bedroom, a woman needs to be emotionally and mentally prepared, often hours in advance. Her preparation requires tender consideration, while harshness or abusive treatment can easily remove her desire for days at a time. When a woman's emotions have been trampled by her husband, she can almost be repulsed by his advances. Many women have told me that they feel like prostitutes when they're forced to make love while feeling resentment toward their husbands. However, a man may have NO idea what he is putting his wife through when he does this.

These basic differences are the source of many conflicts in marriage. And they usually surface soon after the wedding ceremony. The woman intuitively has a greater awareness of how to develop a loving relationship. Because of her sensitivity, initially she is usually more considerate of his feelings and is enthusiastic about developing a meaningful, multilevel relationship: that is, a relationship having more facets than just a sexual partnership. She wants to be a lover, a best friend, a fan, a homemaker, and an appreciated partner. The man, on the other hand, does not generally have her intuitive awareness of what the relationship should become. He doesn't have an intuitive awareness of how to encourage and love his wife or how to treat her in a way that meets her deepest needs.

Since he doesn't have an understanding of these vital areas through intuition, he must rely *solely* upon the knowledge and skills he has acquired in these areas prior to marriage. Unfortunately, our educational system does not provide an adequate training program for a young man before marriage. His only education may be the example he observed in his home. For many of us, that example might have been insufficient. Most men enter marriage knowing everything about sex and very little about genuine, unselfish love. Your example and help may be your husband's only hope for acquiring the knowledge and skills necessary to love you and your children in the way that you need to be loved.

I am not saying men are more selfish than women. I'm simply saying that at the outset of a marriage a man is not as equipped to *express* unselfish love as a woman is. (You and I both know that women can be every bit as self-centered as men.)

INTUITIVE DIFFERENCES

Norman was planning to invest over $50,000 in a business opportunity that was a "sure thing." He had scrutinized the opportunity from every angle and had logically deduced that it couldn't miss. After signing a contract and handing over a check to the other party, he decided it was about time he told his wife about the investment.

Upon hearing a few of the details, she immediately had an uneasy feeling about the deal. When he sensed her uneasiness, Norman became angry and asked her why she felt that way. She couldn't give a logical reason because she didn't have one. All she knew was that it just didn't "sit right." Norman gave in, went back to the other party, and asked for a refund. He was told that he was crazy but was given his money back. A short time later, ALL of the organizers and investors were indicted by the federal government. His wife's intuition had not only saved him $50,000, but it may have kept Norman from going to jail.

What exactly is this "woman's intuition"? It's not something mystical; rather, it is an unconscious perception of minute details that are sometimes tangible, sometimes abstract in nature. Since it is usually an "unconscious" process, many times a woman isn't able to give specific explanations for the way she feels. She simply perceives or "feels" something about a situation or person, while a man tends to follow logical analysis of circumstances or people.

Knowing now that men and women cannot, without an effort, understand each other's differences, I trust that this chapter has given you a little more hope, patience, and tolerance as you endeavor to strengthen and deepen your relationship with your husband. With this in mind, we're ready to begin to discover how you can help your husband become more sensitive.

FOR PERSONAL REFLECTION

List specific ways you differ from your husband in building relationships:
    with each other
    with your children
    with relatives
    with friends
    with your church

4

Helping Your Husband Become
More Sensitive

"A gentle answer turns away wrath, but a harsh word stirs up anger."

Proverbs 15:1

After twenty-five years of being single, Sandy was finally marrying the man of her dreams. Sandy had been dating Larry for four years and thought she knew him inside-out. Their courtship had its ups and downs, but all things considered, she knew their love was so strong that living happily ever after would be as natural as waking up in the morning.

The wedding day finally came, and it was everything she had dreamed about—Larry really was Prince Charming. Then came the honeymoon. Almost immediately she began to see a side of Larry she didn't know existed. On the fourth day of the honeymoon, Larry decided Sandy would enjoy seeing where he used to work in the summers during college. So they began their five-mile hike at the 8,000-foot level of the High Sierras (something every woman dreams of doing on the fourth day of her honeymoon). By the time they arrived at their destination, she was exhausted. Since they had to be back at the lodge by dark, they had time for only a short rest.

By the time they got back to the camp, she had a new concept of physical exhaustion. Prince Charming was tired too, so they immediately went to bed. (Actually, he leaped and she crawled.) To her total amazement, the Prince didn't want to go to sleep—he had more exciting things in mind. From that point on, she began to see marriage as a growing conflict between two self-natures that wanted their own needs met before considering the needs of another.

She had entered marriage thinking Larry would be dedicating himself to meeting her needs. After all, he said in his wedding vows that he would love and cherish her for better or for worse, for rich or for poor, in sickness and in health, until death. In his particular vows, which he had written, he even said he committed himself to provide for all of her needs for the rest of his life. But the vows were quickly becoming mere ceremonial words, and her needs were obviously becoming secondary to his.

She thought she could change him through confrontation by demanding in various ways that he become considerate of her needs. After eight years, things had only become worse. She finally resigned herself to the fact that her relationship with Larry would never improve. Larry, of course, was convinced that the marriage problems were Sandy's fault. He considered her demanding and argumentative. She no longer respected or appreciated him as she had when they were going together.

Today, six years later, Larry is no longer the same self-centered, inconsiderate, demanding husband that he was. Sandy's eyes sparkle when she talks about all the ways he shows his love for her daily, the way he considers her desires even above his own needs. He has become the sensitive husband she always dreamed about. He provides all the strength she'll ever need and yet loves her with gentleness and care. WHAT HAPPENED? Simply stated, Sandy began using five important principles whenever she approached Larry about his insensitivity to her.

No one likes to be criticized, regardless of how much truth lies behind the criticism. Whether we are male or female, six or sixty, when someone corrects us, we automatically become defensive. Yet honest communication is vital to marriage. These two basic truths appear contradictory. How do you honestly tell the one you love about something you find displeasing or aggravating without prompting that familiar, defensive glare or indifferent shrug?

> YOUR HUSBAND CAN BECOME MORE SENSITIVE THROUGH *INDIRECT* METHODS, RATHER THAN THROUGH DIRECT CONFRONTATION

The following five principles outline that indirect approach. A husband is far more apt to receive your comments about his insensitivity when he hears them expressed through these five principles.

1. *Learn to express your feelings through three loving attitudes: warmth, empathy, and sincerity.* These are common words, but what do they mean? Why are they so necessary?

  a. *Warmth* is the friendly acceptance of a person. It's considering a person to be *important* enough to give your time and resources to—to share his concerns, not because he has earned it, but simply because he's a human being.

b. *Empathy* is the ability to understand and identify with a person's feelings—simply being able to put yourself in his shoes and see a situation from his viewpoint.

c. *Sincerity* is showing a genuine concern for a person without changing your attitude toward him when circumstances change.

Your husband may resist your help unless he *sees* these three attitudes within you. These are attitudes that *anyone* can develop. (There is growing evidence in the field of psychology that unless psychiatrists are able to develop these three attitudes within their personalities, their patients will tend to resist their help. In fact, many professionals say that a patient can be helped more by a friend who has these three attitudes than he or she can by a professional who lacks them.)

What happened in Sandy's marriage is now happening in countless marriages, and it *can* happen in yours. The exciting fact is that you *don't have to wait* for your husband to change, even though he may be the primary source of most of the problems. You can start the ball rolling by yourself, and the exciting changes discussed in this book *will* come about!

2. *Learn to share your feelings when angry or irritated WITHOUT using "you" statements.*

Dr. Jerry R. Day, a psychologist from Tucson, Arizona, strongly encourages wives to avoid using "you" statements. For example, "You make me sick" or "You're always late" or "You've always got the answers." "You" statements usually cause a man either to dig in and fight or to promptly leave your presence without resolving the issue. Either way, it makes him more determined to have his own way and causes you to lose ground in the situation.

For example, the statement, "You're never home on time" will tend to cause him to reason, "Who is she to set my schedule; the world doesn't revolve around her—I'll come home anytime I want!"

The statement, "Can't you think about *my* feelings for a change?" makes him think, "Her feelings! What about *my* feelings?"

Or the statement, "Can't you get up earlier and take care of the kids just once?" can cause him to think, "I can't believe how hard I work every day for this family, and now she wants me to do her job."

3. *Learn to WAIT until your anger or feelings of irritability have subsided before you begin to discuss a sensitive issue.*

No matter what you say or how you say it, if you're angry or irritated at the time, it probably will provoke a wrong reaction in him. While you're waiting to cool off, either remain quiet or change the subject to one you can talk about. If your husband wants to know why you're quiet or why you're changing the subject, say to him quietly, "I need a little time to think this through so I can better understand *my* feelings."

(I AM NOT saying that you have to eliminate the feelings of anger from your life. I understand how hard it is to deal with anger. However, when those times arise, avoid discussing a sensitive issue in the heat of anger. That way, neither of you will exchange words you will later regret.)

4. *When you have cooled off, replace "you" statements with "I feel" messages.*

Here are a few examples of what I mean:

Instead of confronting your tardy husband as he walks through the door with, "You never come home on time," greet him with an understanding statement like, "Must have been a hairy day" or "I'll bet you're tired." LATER (maybe even a day or two later, at a time when he's relaxed), begin to share your feelings in the context of your uniqueness as a woman. If you can creatively share your feelings in a positive context, that's even better. For example, "You know, there are some things that you do that really make me feel loved and appreciated, like coming home for dinner on time or letting me know if you'll be late. Those are the ways that you show your love for me. I really need that."

Instead of waking your husband with the words, "Can't you get up early and help me take care of the kids just once?" wait until a time when he's not tired and try something like this: "You work so hard for this family. I wish I had your stamina so I wouldn't need your help in the mornings, but I really need your help or I'm afraid I'm not going to have what it takes to meet your needs. And taking care of you is becoming more important to me than ever before." Or . . . "You work so hard for this family, I hate to ask anything else of you. But I do know something you could do that would make me feel extra-special. Often it's difficult for me to handle the pressure of getting the kids ready for school. It would really make me feel like I'm special if you could help me take care of the kids before school."

By learning to share your feelings calmly, you will gradually wear down his tendency to react sharply in anger. It may take time, but if you persist, you will see changes. The principle that "A gentle answer turns away wrath" (Prov. 15:1) really works as long as your soft answer is not said with a self-righteous or sarcastic attitude.

You should keep sharing your feelings until he understands. You may have to tell him over and over again for weeks that something he does makes you feel worthless. At first he'll defend his actions or tell you why your feelings aren't warranted or logical. Just keep telling him that you're not trying to justify your feelings; you're just trying to explain them honestly to him. Whether he thinks they're logical or not doesn't change the fact that you have those exact feelings. You are unique, and even if you were the only person in the whole world with those feelings, he still needs to understand how you feel.

5. *Abandon "I told you so" statements.*

Such statements can take many forms and should be completely eliminated. They reflect arrogance and self-centeredness, and only set your marriage relationship back. Here are some of the more typical ways of saying "I told you so."

"If you had done what I asked you to do . . ."

"I knew it!"

"Just like I thought."

"I only asked you to do one thing and . . ."

"I can't believe you."

"You never listen, do you?"

"Seeeeeeeee?"

"You always have to do it your way, don't you?"

"Well, I hope you're satisfied."

"I'm not going to say it. . . ."

"Maybe some day you'll take *my* advice."

List at least five ways that you have said, "I told you so."

1._____

2._____
3._____
4._____
5._____

As you begin to apply some of the principles discussed in this chapter, you may encounter a bit of failure and frustration. Some of your noblest efforts may be criticized or ridiculed, but don't give up. There is an age-old principle I see proved every day in marriages all over the nation: You reap what you sow. If you persist in developing and expressing the qualities in this chapter, you will ultimately see those same qualities developed in your husband.

Dr. Howard Hendricks says studies reveal that children are more likely to follow their parents' ideals and instructions because of what they see their parents *are* rather than because of what they hear their parents *say*. I believe the same principle applies with the husband-wife relationship. When he sees the qualities in your life that you desire for him, he will be motivated to make those same qualities a part of his life.

FOR PERSONAL REFLECTION

Write out ten gentle phrases you could use during irritating times with your mate, such as those times when he uses your shaver or promises to run an errand. Remember Proverbs 15:1.

5

Motivating Your Husband To Listen To You

"The Lord's bond-servant must not be quarrelsome, but be kind to all, able to teach . . ." (emphasis mine).
2 Timothy 2:24

Lois had a pretty good marriage by today's standards. She considered her husband a good provider and an excellent father. However, the romance had faded from their marriage, and her feelings of affection toward Mark were very inconsistent. She decided she would do all she could to make her marriage what she wanted it to be. She began reading various books on what she could do to be a better wife and was gaining enthusiasm each day.

After several weeks, she stumbled across two books written for men, telling them what they could do to strengthen their marriages. She brought them home for Mark and decided to give them to him after dinner. The moment of truth finally came. She walked over to Mark with a sweet smile and said, "Honey, I've really been working hard lately to learn how to become a better wife so I can be what you deserve to have. I found two books that can help a husband better understand his wife. Would you read them for me?"

FOR BETTER

Mark gave her a condescending look and said, "We'll see."

Not giving up at that sure sign of defeat, she said, a little more defensively, "I've been reading a lot of books lately and really working hard to make our marriage better. This is the least you can do."

Mark gave excuse number four on man's "Ten Most Widely Used Excuses" list. He simply said, "Sweetie, you know how busy I am these days. I'll really try when my schedule slows down." She knew that could be a while, because in two years of marriage she had never seen his schedule "slow down."

But there was something Lois could have said that would have motivated Mark to read both books within three nights. In fact, he probably would have taken time off work to finish them the next day.

This principle is not given to be used as a manipulative tool. Manipulation usually results in anger, hurt, worry, fear, and other negative emotions, but genuine love causes joy and fulfillment. Manipulation can't wait to get, and love can't wait to give. If your motive for using this principle is based on love, on enriching your husband's life, it can help you enter into a more loving, attentive conversation with him. You'll be able to search out his deepest needs and selflessly dedicate yourself to meeting those needs.

It's called the "salt principle." Salt makes people thirsty, and the goal of this principle is to create a thirst for constructive conversation in which both you and your husband can learn about each other's needs.

Simply stated, the principle is this:

NEVER COMMUNICATE INFORMATION
YOU CONSIDER TO BE IMPORTANT
WITHOUT FIRST CREATING A BURNING
CURIOSITY WITHIN THE LISTENER.

This principle is so easy to learn that even a child can master it. One day my seven-year-old daughter came running into the house crying. I called her over and asked what was wrong. She told me that her little girlfriend never listened to her. Every time Kari would start to tell her girlfriend something, the friend would interrupt and start talking. Kari told me she felt like she didn't have anything important to say because her friend would never listen.

I asked Kari if she would like to learn a way that would make her friend want to listen to her. She was all ears as she hopped up into my lap, and I asked her, "What were some of the things you wanted to say to your friend?"

She replied, "I wanted to tell her what I did with my dollhouse, but she didn't want to hear."

I told Kari that first she had to get her friend's attention with a statement or two that would make her friend want to hear more. She would have to make these statements with *enthusiasm.* We decided she could say something like, "You won't believe *what I did* to my new dollhouse!" Then she would pause and come back with a second statement, "My *parents* couldn't even believe what I did with it."

When I came home from work the following evening, Kari was all smiles. She told me that our plan had worked so well that her girlfriend not only listened to her, but came over and played with the dollhouse.

FOR BETTER

Obviously, for adults the situations are more complicated, although the principle remains the same. Arouse their curiosity and you've got their attention!

Faye was worried because Jack was too busy to spend time with their son Randy.

Jack's work schedule kept him so busy that he spent very little time with Randy when he was home. Fay realized how much their son needed him, but Jack was usually too preoccupied to listen. Faye decided to give the salt principle a try, and here's how it went:

Faye: (salt)	I heard some very discouraging news from school today about Randy.
Jack:	Oh, no, what was it?
Faye: (more salt)	I don't know what we're going to do about it . . . I'm really worried.
Jack:	Well, what is it?
Faye: (big salt)	Unless you can help out, it will probably end up *costing us* a lot of money.
Jack:	Faye, what are you talking about?
Faye: (The words "special help" begin to resalt for the next thing she's going to say.)	Randy's teacher called and said Randy has a reading problem. Unless he gets *special help*, it could handicap him for the rest of his education.
Jack:	What do you mean "special help"?
Faye:	The teacher explained that if you or I

didn't do something about it, we would probably have to pay a lot of money to have it corrected later. She said the longer it goes uncorrected, the worse it will become.

Jack: What could we do now?

Faye: Well, there's not too much I can do,
(salt)   but she did say there was something you could do.

Jack: What's that?

Faye: In fact, she said if you would do it con-
(more salt)   sistently, it would provide just what he needs to whip the problem. I told her you were very busy and I didn't know if you could find the time . . .

Jack: I'll make the time . . . what is it?

Faye: She said that the basis of the problem involves motor skills. If you could do something like beginning to throw the football with him consistently, his hand/eye coordination would increase and she would be able to help him get his reading up to par.

Today, four years later, Jack still plays football with Randy. Jack not only enjoys their time together, but he also has the satisfaction of knowing that he has done something to help Randy in school that no one else could have done. All of this was a result of Faye's taking the time to creatively communicate a genuine need using the salt principle.

Knowing that you need to arouse his curiosity is one thing, but actually doing it is quite another, right? You're probably wondering, "So now what? How do I apply the salt principle to my circumstances?"

Let's examine the principle a little further to see what it really means.

HOW TO CATCH YOUR HUSBAND'S INTEREST AND KEEP IT

1. *The first step is to clearly identify the need or concern you wish to communicate to your husband.*

In our first illustration, Lois wanted Mark to learn more about what a woman needs from a man, and, more precisely, she wanted him to read the two books she had just purchased for him on the subject. In the second illustration, Faye wanted Jack to begin spending more time with Randy.

2. *The second step is to identify related areas that are of high interest to your husband.*

This is where Lois failed and Faye succeeded. Lois simply communicated what she was interested in (a happier marriage) but failed to relate her interest to any of her husband's interests. He could not see that he needed any help in becoming a better husband, so becoming a better husband was not of particular interest to him.

Faye, on the other hand, succeeded on this point. She knew her husband's business schedule was of greater interest to him than spending time with Randy. However, she also knew from past discussions that he was extremely interested in their son's education. She identified that interest and remembered Randy's teacher's comments about his reading problem. Since a big part of Randy's problem was his hand/eye coordination, she figured anything Jack could play with Randy to increase his hand/eye coordination would help solve the problem. And then she thought of football. She saw how she could relate Jack's interest (Randy's education) to her interest (wanting to see Jack and Randy have more time together) and also see Randy's reading problem corrected.

Lois didn't have to fail on this point with Mark. Having been married only two years, Mark has told me that his sexual appetite is much greater than Lois's (which is usually the case). I am sure Lois was aware of Mark's high interest in increasing her sexual desires. This is the area of *high interest* she could have used to increase his interest in reading the two books. In the next steps I'll show you how she could have accomplished this.

3. *Using his area of high interest, share enough information to stimulate his curiosity to hear more.*

Since Lois knew of Mark's never-ending physical drive, she could have started with the statement, "I can't believe these two books! I began reading them while you were at work, and I started to get so turned-on I had to put them down. I was really wishing you were home so we could make love."

Knowing Mark, I guarantee that she would have had his undivided attention. Even the Super Bowl would have been turned off at this point.

4. *Add a little more salt. Don't answer his response to your first dose of salt; rather, pause and build his curiosity even more.*

Mark probably would have responded to the first dose with one of the following:

—You're kidding. What did it say?

—Really? Let me see it.

—It's not too late. I'm home now.

Now Lois applies her second dose of salt, *without* giving any relief to Mark's budding curiosity, with a statement like this: "They really are unbelievable. They tell a man just what he needs to do to prepare his wife mentally and emotionally for sex. Those authors really understand what it takes to turn me on."

5. *Use a short question to gain a commitment to his pursuit of your interest or to teach him what you're trying to communicate.*

Lois, at this point, can gain a commitment from Mark to read the first book by asking him one of several short questions: "Have you ever read a book like this that tells you the five things that women can't resist?" or "Have you ever read about the five things you can do that turn me on?"

Lois's goal was not to turn her husband into a manipulator of her sexual desires, but to get him to read two books that would encourage him to do the things that would build up their emotional relationship. She knew the "five things" would motivate her husband to treat her with greater tenderness and respect which, in turn, would help her to be more sexually responsive.

6. *After you have taken these five steps, if he still doesn't show sufficient interest or commitment, keep adding salt.*

Lois could further salt with a statement like, "I'm glad you haven't learned any of these yet; my sexual drive would probably get so strong we'd never get any work done around here."

As I said at the beginning of this chapter, the salt principle is irresistible if used correctly. Every aspect of loving and communicating can be used either beneficially or detrimentally—the salt principle is no different. To use it effectively, there are a few things you definitely want to avoid.

OR FOR BEST
"WHAT NOT-TO-DO" WHEN SALTING!

1. *Do not begin the conversation with a plea or request for his attention or time.*

When you are going to use the salt principle, never start the conversation with statements like the following:

—Can I see you for a minute?

—I really need to talk to you!

—Can we talk about something really important a little later?

—I've been waiting a long time to talk to you. Can we *please* talk tonight?

Introductory statements like these usually generate a negative response because some husbands can't visualize setting aside time "just to talk." Chances are, you'll get hurt from his lack of interest. The dialogue below shows a typical example:

Alice: I would really like to talk to you about a few things after dinner tonight. Okay, dear?

Fred: There's a game on tonight that I've really been counting on seeing. Besides, I've got some work to catch up on.

Alice: Well, how about when you're done? This is really important.

Fred: Look, I'd like to talk, but it's been a tough day and I'm really tired. Maybe tomorrow.

Alice: There's always something else . . . you never want to spend time with me. . . .

And from there the fight is on. Instead of using an introductory statement, start out with a statement that creates curiosity.

2. *Do not start your conversation with your main concern or your solution.*

For example, if Faye had opened her conversation with the statement below, she would have evoked a different response from Jack.

Faye: Dear, Randy needs more of your time, and throwing a football would help his reading problem. Could you start playing football with him?

Jack: I'd love to play with my son, but I just don't have time. You know my schedule.

3. *Don't try to persuade him with your first few statements.*

Often women tend to think the only way they can get their insensitive husbands to do something is to shove them into action with a strong statement or threat. This may work for the short-range, but it can cause him to hear "Wolf! Wolf!"

Faye: Dear, you have to start spending more time with Randy or else there're going to be real problems.

Jack: Don't tell me what I have to do. I don't have time to play with him and do my job too. Why don't I quit work, and I'll stay home all day? Then I'll have *lots* of time to play with him.

DON'T GIVE UP! SALTING REALLY WORKS, EVEN WHEN A PERSON KNOWS WHAT YOU ARE DOING

If you don't succeed the first time you use the salt principle, don't give up. You may have to use it several times before you become skilled at it, but given time and practice, it will work! I've never met anyone who couldn't do it as long as he or she just kept trying. Surprisingly, it works even if the other person knows what you are doing.

Use the following exercise to help you tailor this principle to some of your immediate needs and concerns. Also, the principle of "salting" will be more solidified in your own thinking if you take some time to do this.

1. *List four of your current needs or concerns that you would like your husband to understand more fully.*

(For example: a material need, your feeling about someone, an activity you would like to do with him, or a "hurt" that you want him to understand.)

1._____
2._____
3._____
4._____

EXAMPLE:
  1. *My feelings about his mother*
  2. *My fear of moving again*
  3. *My need for understanding instead of lectures*
  4. *My need for more companionship with him*

2. *List five areas that are of very high interest to your husband.*

(For example: hobbies, business projects, career and related interests, religious concerns, friends, sports, TV programs.)

1._____
2._____
3._____
4._____
5._____

FOR BETTER

EXAMPLE:

1. *Success in business*
2. *Sexual fulfillment*
3. *Concern for the total welfare of the children*
4. *Acceptance among the men at his office*
5. *Relationship with God*

3. Write down at least two statements or questions that would create curiosity about one of your four concerns or needs.

Try to relate it to one of his five areas of high interest.

1._____
2._____

EXAMPLE:

1. *Do you know what psychologists say is the greatest deter-mining factor in the emotional stability of a child?*

2. *If you and I would decide to work on this together, not only would our children gain emotional stability, but I would probably develop a stronger sexual desire just by being around you.*

She is talking about her need for companionship *and* she is relating it to two important areas of his life—his concern for their children's welfare and his desire for greater sexual fulfillment. In this example, the wife had remembered that she had read that children become better balanced when they see consistent affection and warmth between their parents. She tied all of this together and created two "salty" statements.

OR FOR BEST

The more you use the salting principle, the more effective you will become in applying it. You'll find that it not only works with your husband, but with anyone whom you want to listen to you with undivided attention.

FOR PERSONAL REFLECTION

What example did Jesus give us of the salt principle? He never wasted His time sharing important truths with people who were not interested. He even taught against teaching truth to the disinterested (Matt. 7:6). Jesus used parables and questions to arouse curiosity.

6

Motivating Your Husband To Change

"If any of them (husbands) are disobedient to the word, they may be won without a word by the behavior of their wives" (emphasis mine).

1 Peter 3:1

How many times have you tried to tell your husband that you need to be loved emotionally during the day-to-day routine if he wants you to enter wholeheartedly into intimacy with him? You need gentleness, affection, thoughtfulness, and romance *before* you go to the bedroom if you are to give of yourself unreservedly *in* the bed. In the same manner, he must see certain qualities in your life that make him *aware* of your needs and receptive to your feelings before he can respond to those needs and feelings.

Because a man may enter marriage with such a low level of knowledge and skill to meet a woman's needs, it is essential that his wife teach him what her needs and feelings are and, ultimately, show him how he can meet those needs. He becomes far more receptive to learning about your needs and how he can fulfill them when *six qualities* are present in your life.

All six are probably present in your character to one de-

55

gree or another and, if they are nourished, they will grow stronger and have a greater influence on your personality. As this growth takes place, your husband will have a much greater desire to learn how to love you in the way you need to be loved.

> THERE ARE SIX ESSENTIAL INNER-BEAUTY QUALITIES THAT PREPARE A HUSBAND TO LISTEN.

When you were in school, you may have noticed that some courses were much more enjoyable than others simply because they were taught by an instructor you liked. It was easier and more enjoyable to learn from teachers who possessed certain character qualities.

When the qualities of courage, persistence, gratefulness, calmness, gentleness, and unselfish love are present in a person's character, it is easier to receive his or her words and to follow his or her instruction or example. This is no less true for your marriage. These qualities must be present in some degree before your husband will really want to learn from you.

COURAGE

Courage is the inner commitment to pursue a worthwhile goal without giving up hope.

Many women have ALREADY given up hope that their marriages will ever be any better. When a woman's hope for a better marriage has faded, her attractiveness to her husband diminishes and the "life" of the relationship gradually declines.

Regardless of how discouraged you may be, however, it is *never* too late to rekindle your hope and bring renewed life into your relationship with your husband.

Joyce and Greg had been married for three years. Joyce was pregnant with their first child when she discovered Greg was seeing another woman. Her affections had already begun to fade before she found out about the other woman, and when his affair came to light, her affections died completely. Their relationship went from love, to hate, to indifference.

One day at lunch she broke the usual silence and asked Greg what he was thinking about. With two words he shattered what little hope she had left. "About her," he responded. After he went back to work, she told God that she had no hope left. But she didn't stop there. She went on to pray that if He could give her hope or give her a new love for Greg, she would receive it.

To her surprise, she found herself doing kind little things for Greg, even though she didn't like him. Within three weeks, Greg began to notice such a change in Joyce that he found himself more attracted to her than to the other woman. He even felt ashamed for the way he had been treating her. He broke off his relationship with the other woman and joined Joyce in her growing commitment to build a more fulfilling relationship with each other and with Christ. For Joyce, courage began when she told God that she was *willing* to receive a new hope and love for Greg.

Both Joyce and Greg tell me that their relationship now is so much deeper they can't even imagine how empty it used to be.

The *first step* toward increasing your courage is to commit yourself to *pursue actively* a more fulfilling relationship with your husband and to build a better marriage. One major roadblock to a happy marriage is maintaining unrealistic views of what a good marriage is. These unrealistic views begin in childhood and culminate with the wedding ceremony. That's why psychologists say that when you and your husband said "I do," SIX people were united in marriage.

On the bride's side stood
1. The person you thought you were
2. The person he thought you were
3. The person you ACTUALLY were

On the groom's side stood
1. The person he thought he was
2. The person you thought he was
3. The person he ACTUALLY was

The growth and joy in marriage come from combining these six different expectations into a unified, realistic relationship. And, yes, it *is* possible, and it *can* be done. That's what learning to love is all about, and that's exactly what you are learning as you read this book. Couples who've been married for years have as much to gain in their relationships as do newlyweds.

One newlywed recently told me that when she married her husband she thought she was marrying one of the last sensitive men alive. Within a year, she learned he was not at all as sensitive or "naturally romantic" as she had thought. She thought he had sneaked out and had brain surgery that altered the part of the brain that affected behavior. Before marriage, it seemed as if his considerate ways of caring for her flowed naturally from his inner being. Now she is disappointed and even irritated that such actions are not a natural part of his manner. In fact, he has to stop and think about how to carry out even the smallest acts of kindness. When she voices her discontent, he gives her a puzzled look and asks, "What am I supposed to do?" Like most women, she is further irritated because she feels, "If I have to tell him what to do, it takes all of the meaning out of it!"

I've heard her story repeated hundreds of times. That's why it is important to have a clear mental picture of what constitutes a good marriage. Rather than having me tell you what I think a good marriage is, let me do something a little different. Which of the following would make your marriage what *you* would like it to be? Check as many as you like.

My marriage would be much better if my husband . . .

☐ would make me feel respected and more important than his work, his relatives, his friends, and his pastimes.

☐ would really try to understand my feelings and needs and learn how to respond lovingly to them.

☐ would genuinely desire and seek forgiveness when he hurts my feelings or the children's feelings

☐ would consistently feel and express sincere appreciation for who I am and what I do.

☐ would recognize my sensitivity as a strength and welcome my encouragement for him to become more sensitive.

☐ would understand my unique physical limitations and enthusiastically take an active part in dealing with the children and household responsibilities.

☐ would allow me to lean on him emotionally for comfort when discouraged or distressed, without criticism or lectures.

☐ would respect me enough to *welcome* my opinions and advice when making decisions that affect our family.

☐ would want to be my best friend and would want me to be his.

☐ would not try to impose values and ideals upon me that he is not applying himself, eliminating any double standard.

Each one of these descriptions is a worthwhile *attainable* goal. In the chapters that follow, each is discussed in detail. You will be given precise steps of action that you can begin to take immediately to make these goals a reality in your marriage.

While the first step toward increasing your courage is to commit yourself to an active pursuit of a better marriage, the *second step* is to commit yourself to *endure the pressure* that may come from your husband as you begin to pursue a better marriage, keeping in mind that his desire to enrich your marriage is probably far less at this point than yours.

Shortly after their wedding, Denise was shocked at the difference between Jerry's behavior as a husband and as a boyfriend. She became discouraged, but after joining a group of couples with whom I meet, she made a commitment to pursue a better marriage. For the first few months, she encountered increased pressure and resistance from Jerry. One day when she was sick, she tried to share her feelings of weakness with him, telling him how much she needed his comfort and help around the house. His offhand reply was, "Oh, come on, gut it up . . . you can do it." He went on to imply that his mother never acted that way when *she* was sick.

Jerry didn't change overnight. On another occasion, Denise (a schoolteacher) asked him to visit her school to see how she and her students had decorated the classroom. It had taken a lot of work and creativity on her part, and she was really proud of the results. Once again, Prince Charming rose to the occasion by sarcastically saying, "I don't ask you to come see my office. Why make me come see your classroom? Besides, if you've seen one classroom, you've seen them all."

But the story didn't end with Jerry's sarcasm. Because Denise had made the second commitment, "to endure the pressure that comes from pursuing a better marriage," Jerry has changed. He has entered into the same commitment to build a better marriage. He is becoming more and more sensitive to Denise and now takes an active part in assuming many of the household responsibilities. That alone has helped draw them much closer. He's beginning to respect Denise, her unique qualities, and her unique sensitivities.

You may or may not encounter pressure or resistance as you begin a more active pursuit of a better marriage, but it's important that you commit yourself to endure any pressure that may come. If you wait for him to initiate a better relationship, it may be a long, long wait.

PERSISTENCE

Persistence means continuing to pursue a goal until it is achieved.

For years, Ken's way of dealing with Carla's hurt feelings was to give her a lecture on or a rational explanation for why she was hurting and how she could stop. These ranged in length from the brief "you're too sensitive" all the way to the twenty-minute complex analysis of her entire situation. Carla always assumed it was just his way of trying to tell her he was superior by making her feel at fault. If someone didn't talk to her at the party and she deduced they didn't like her anymore, Ken would simply tell her, "Oh, they were just too busy . . . you're just taking it too seriously." If she had an argument with his mother, his mother got his understanding while Carla got comments like, "You overreacted," or "I can't believe how you hurt Mom's feelings."

After Carla realized that men have to learn how to respond to women's feelings, she began to tell Ken each time she needed comfort, "Don't lecture me . . . just hold me and understand." This didn't do a bit of good the first six or seven times she tried it. She still got his lectures (although they kept getting shorter). Finally Ken (genius that he is), realized that Carla was simply asking him not to preach at her but to comfort her with silent gentleness. He tried it once and noticed a completely different response in Carla. She recovered from her hurt feelings much faster than when he tried to explain away her feelings.

Ken told me that although it was hard not to lecture the first few times, his quiet response was so much more effective that it has now become natural. If Carla had tried to help him change by sharing her feelings only once, nothing would have happened. But she persisted, and now both she and Ken are enjoying the benefits of her persistence.

Several years ago I met a man who had been very successful in his work with teenagers. He had influenced thousands of young people in a positive way. When I asked him the secret of his success, I was surprised by his answer. He said, "It's simple. For every 200 ideas I try, one works!" One of the teenagers from his youth group, Jill, followed his example after she married.

Since the first week of their marriage, Jill had noticed how Dave always showed preference for his family over hers. When they moved across the country for Dave to attend graduate school, she thought she would be free of rating second to his family. Unfortunately, 2,000 miles wasn't far enough. Phone calls, letters, or visits with the family continued to add fuel to the fire. Whenever Jill found fault with any of Dave's family, Dave would always rise to their defense. Time after time she would try to tell Dave how deeply it bothered her that he preferred his family over her, but Dave always defended himself.

A few years after graduate school, Dave finally had the chance to relocate near their hometown. He thought Jill would be thrilled because it meant living near her family too. He couldn't understand why she cried when he told her about the opportunity. Once again she explained that she was afraid to live near his family because of his preference for them. As usual, he defended himself and couldn't see it from her viewpoint.

On vacation they visited their hometown. As they were leaving his family, he asked her, "Tell me one more time why you don't want to move back?" She explained once more, and it finally got through. Since then, he has had many opportunities to demonstrate his preference for Jill. She now feels so secure that she is looking forward to the possibility of returning home. Once again, the wife's gentle persistence brought lasting benefit to her and her husband.

GRATEFULNESS

Gratefulness is a sincere appreciation for the benefits you have gained from others.

A survey was recently taken among several thousand workers, asking what their employers could do to motivate them to work harder. The employers were amazed that the number-one response had nothing to do with income or benefits. The majority of workers stated that *the one thing* their employers did to make them want to work harder was to *express appreciation* for their individual efforts.

63

FOR BETTER

If gratefulness motivates a person to try harder on the job, why won't it motivate your husband to try harder in the home? The answer is, IT WILL! Gratefulness expressed through praise is one of the highest motivations for men. If you want your relationship with your husband to become more fulfilling, it is essential that you develop a grateful attitude.

Praise expressed from a grateful heart is essential to our walk with God. We actually enter into His presence through praise (Ps. 100:4); and our faith in Him is proven through our willingness to thank Him in all circumstances, no matter how destructive we may think they could be (1 Thess. 5:18; Rom. 8:28). We haven't learned to walk with Christ until we learn to say "thank You, Lord, for 'that.' I don't understand it, but I trust that You can work it for my good because I love You."

Kathy and John had been married for eighteen years. When Kathy came to my office, she was distressed because John was an alcoholic. In spite of the problems that resulted from his alcoholism, she was still committed to pursuing a better marriage. I told her that gratefulness expressed through praise could provide a powerful motivation for John to overcome his problem. We also talked about the other qualities discussed in this chapter, and how she could develop them in her life. When she left my office, she had an enthusiastic desire to begin practicing some of the steps immediately.

Several weeks later there was a knock at my door, and when I opened it I had to catch my breath. To my surprise John had come up to my office to talk with me. He told me that since his wife had come to see me there had been so many changes in her life that she was like a new person. He went on to say, "She's become so loving and appreciative, I just can't go on hurting her anymore. Would you help me?"

This couple's story graphically illustrates the power of these inner qualities and, more specifically, the power of gratefulness to motivate a man to want a better relationship. You may be wondering what qualities Kathy found to be praiseworthy in her alcoholic husband. She used her greatest strength to detect these qualities.

USING YOUR GREATEST STRENGTH TO DETECT PRAISEWORTHY QUALITIES IN YOUR HUSBAND

It should be evident by now that a woman's greatest strength is her sensitivity. Sensitivity can become your best friend in your effort to detect admirable qualities in your husband. When I first mentioned to Kathy that she needed to express gratefulness to John, she gave me a bewildered look and said, "What's there to be grateful for? Do you know what it's like to live with an alcoholic?" I explained to her that there are many positive qualities that can have negative expressions. We talked about a few of her husband's negative traits in order to detect some positive qualities she could begin to praise.

The most obvious problem she could think of was his self-pity. Self-pity can be a negative expression of compassion, so I asked Kathy if she had ever sensed that John was concerned for the welfare of others. Her eyes lit up immediately. She said she had always noticed how quick he was to show concern for those who had misfortunes.

I asked her if she had ever noticed whether he was sneaky about hiding a bottle or getting away for a drink. Once again she smiled. Craftiness is often a negative expression of creativity. (One of the most creative men I ever read about had been a thief for more than twenty years.) When I explained that craftiness and creativity are often different expressions of the same characteristic, she told me that John's job required a great deal of creativity. In a matter of minutes we had picked out two qualities for which she could begin to praise him. In order for her praise to be sincere, she would need to use her sensitivity to detect the proper times and opportunities to express praise. (NOTE: The following list may help you use some of your husband's negative traits to discern his admirable qualities.)

Negative Behavior	Positive Characteristics
Slow	Cautious, attentive to detail
Careless	Easy-going, lenient
Fussy	Careful, likes to do things right or "first class"
Can't say "No"	Peace-loving, gentle with people, compassionate, helpful
Talks too much	Thorough, expressive
Too strict	Disciplined, self-controlled, thorough
Pushy	Determined, aggressive, persuasive

DEVELOPING A GRATEFUL ATTITUDE

The *first step* in developing a genuine attitude of gratefulness is becoming aware that the benefits in your life have come from two main sources: other people and God. When confronted with this idea, one man said that it simply was not true. He started in business with nothing and had become extremely wealthy. He said, "No one ever gave me anything." He was asked how far he could have gone in business if he hadn't learned to read or write. His obvious reply was, "Not far." Then he lowered his eyes and acknowledged that someone else had offered him an invaluable asset that he had used most of his life. Before he knew it, he could think of dozens of people from whom he had received countless benefits.

If you stop to think about it, there are very few benefits in your life for which you can take sole credit. Before going any further, take time to complete the following exercise.

Developing Gratefulness Exercise #1

In column A list ten of the most treasured benefits in your life. (For example: your children, education, talents, material possessions, abilities.) In column B list the name of at least one person who contributed to the corresponding benefit listed in column A.

COLUMN A	COLUMN B
Ex. My children	EX. Husband
	Dr. Shaughnessy, Nurse
1. _____	1. _____
2. _____	2. _____

3. _____   3. _____

4. _____   4. _____

5. _____   5. _____

6. _____   6. _____

7. _____   7. _____

8. _____   8. _____

9. _____   9. _____

10. _____   10. _____

The *second step* in developing a grateful attitude is learning to minimize your expectations of your spouse. Expectations can be one of the most destructive forces in your marriage. They can bring unnecessary disappointment and discouragement to you and your husband.

Imagine that you have no money in savings and are suddenly hit with a hospital bill of $2,000. Banks and finance companies turn you down, but a friend agrees to give you a loan. You promise to pay it back in six months. Six months later when you have just saved enough to pay your friend back, you are hit with another bill. So, you spend what you've saved and have nothing left to pay back the debt. Ten days later your friend calls and asks, "Where's the money?" You explain what happened, and she says, "You promised to pay me back in six months, so get me the money," and she hangs up. Chances are, you'd look for the nearest bottle of Pepto-Bismol.

The next day your friend calls back to ask if you have the money yet, saying she needs it desperately. When you tell her that you still don't have it, she cries and says she's going to call every day until you send the money. By this time, not even Pepto-Bismol will help.

And yet, this is the position in which you place your husband with your expectations. You are constantly holding a debt over his head that he cannot pay because he does not have the resources.

For eight years Ben had been living under the weight of Sue's expectations. Each time he bought her something, either it wasn't enough or it was too late. When he would finally fulfill her expectation, she would express the attitude, "It's about time." He felt like no matter what he did he could never please her. Then Sue stopped expressing her expectations and began expressing appreciation for *any* attempt Ben made to please her. Ben didn't realize what was happening at first, but after a couple of months it dawned on him that he couldn't remember the last time Sue had asked for anything, especially furniture for their home. He was so encouraged by her change in attitude that he bought a whole houseful of furniture, exceeding any of her former expectations.

Ben wasn't the only one who found a new joy as a result of Sue's diminished expectations. Sue discovered that fewer expectations increased her happiness because she allowed her husband the freedom to surprise her.

The best way I know of decreasing your expectations is to change your focus from your husband to God. Psalm 62:1–2 gives us the freedom to expect life from God alone; and Philippians 4:19 assures us that our God will supply all our *needs* through His riches in glory in Christ Jesus. (Those two verses have allowed Norma to take her focus off me meeting her needs and put it onto God meeting her needs.) As we rest in Him, we become free to help those around us because we're not expecting anything from human sources, but only from the Lord.

FOR BETTER

By diminishing your expectations, you can free your husband of a burden that you force him to bear, and you can free yourself from unnecessary disappointment. Diminishing your expectations does not mean getting rid of your needs or wants. That is humanly impossible. It simply means eliminating your time limit and preconceived ideas about when and how those expectations will be fulfilled. The following exercise may help you keep tabs on your expectations.

Developing Gratefulness
Exercise #2

Make a list of your expectations under each category.

Your Material Needs

Ex. New Sofa

_____

_____

_____

_____

His Attitudes

Ex. Impatient with children

_____

_____

_____

Your Emotional Needs

Ex. Praise for a good meal

His Habits

Ex. Throws dirty clothes on floor

_____

_____

_____

_____

OR FOR BEST

The expectations you listed above are like bombs set to destroy your relationship. The only way to deactivate them is to *get rid of the timer.*

CALMNESS

Calmness is an inner peace that allows you to respond quietly to a stressful situation without fear.

Let's go back to the analogy of the butterfly and the buffalo. The butterfly is delicate and sensitive even to the slightest breeze. The buffalo, on the other hand, isn't even bothered by a thirty-mile-an-hour wind. Although your sensitivity is one of your greatest strengths (because it allows you to "feel" things so much more intensely), it can also be a source of discouragement and despair if you do not balance it with calmness.

I'm not even beginning to imply that you should do anything to reduce your sensitivity. In fact, if your husband has succeeded in making you more calloused, it is important that you regain the sensitivity you have lost. The more sensitive you are, the more beauty, gentleness, tenderness, and "feeling" you can bring to your family and your environment.

At the same time, however, because you are aware of what's going on around you, you may easily react to the slightest changes. When we over-react to a situation, we sometimes can cause greater problems than the ones to which we are reacting.

With a car full of noisy Girl Scouts, Jenny was driving on a rain-slick highway, taking them to their meeting. A cat started to run out in front of the car; Jenny over-reacted and swerved radically to avoid it. The car started fishtailing back and forth across the highway until it slammed into a ditch.

Several children were injured, but she had missed the cat. A minor adjustment with the wheel would have enabled her to miss the cat and still maintain control of the car, but she over-reacted to the situation.

The same thing can happen on your "emotional" highway. Your sensitivity enables you to "see" many potential problems that your husband may overlook. You may sense your daughter's hurt feelings when your husband uses harsh words to correct her, while he may be totally unaware that he has even wounded her. Correctly used, your sensitivity can enable you to be aware of your daugther's reaction and, in the right way at the right time, to provide her with the needed comfort. Eventually, it will even enable you to teach your husband how to detect such hurts and, by example, teach him how to bring healing.

The wrong way to use your sensitivity in this situation would be to quickly over-react by criticizing your husband in front of your daughter or by defending her action which provoked his correction in the first place. The first step in developing a calm attitude is to *control* your tendency to over-react.

After thirteen years of marriage, Frank and Evelyn were finally going to have their dream trip to a South Sea island. They were especially excited because part of their expenses were being paid. Three weeks before the trip, Frank learned that the expenses would be far greater than he had anticipated. The meals would be especially costly, but he didn't worry about it because he figured, "How much can we eat anyway?"

When Frank called Evelyn and casually mentioned this, Evelyn did not take it quite as calmly. She knew from past experience that when it came to vacations, Frank was so tight with his wallet that he squeaked. She immediately envisioned all the other couples going to fancy restaurants and Polynesian luaus, while she and Frank would sit in their room feasting on peanut butter sandwiches and a carton of milk. *Without any explanation of how she was feeling,* her reply to Frank was, "I really don't think I want to go."

In the past, Frank would have responded to such a statement with, "If that's the way you feel, we'll cancel the trip." An argument would have followed, and her *over-reaction* probably would have cost them the trip of their dreams. However, this did not happen. Frank was learning to be sensitive to his wife, so he responded to her statement with the question, "Why do you feel that way?" Evelyn was able to *calmly express* her concerns, and Frank assured her that if she would like, she could carry the money designated for meals and they would dine wherever she liked.

Over-reacting not only decreases your husband's desire to meet your needs, but it also forces you to go through many problems that could otherwise be avoided.

The second step in balancing your sensitivity with calmness is to realize that the relationship principles discussed in this book *will* bring about a change. These principles have worked for thousands of couples, including many whose situations appeared very hopeless. At this point, you and many other readers may be saying, "There is no situation more hopeless than mine." You may be right, but see if yours is worse than Mike and Gail's.

The only way to describe Mike and Gail's marriage was "who hates who the most?" They only stayed together because they didn't have enough money to live apart. They had no feelings of love toward their two children. They viewed them as two mistakes who came along and messed up their lifestyle. Each day after work Mike would stop at a bar, meet another woman, go out and get drunk, and come home late at night. Each night he and Gail would have violent fights with Gail coming out on the losing end since Mike was 6'2" and 190 pounds. Gail's greatest hope in life was to have enough money someday to leave Mike and the kids.

One day someone told Gail how she could gain a genuine, lasting love for Mike. She was also told how she could begin to develop inner qualities and express those qualities in a way that would motivate Mike to go through similar changes. She began to apply a simple but life-changing principle. Nothing changed the first week, but by the end of the second week Mike had noticed such a radical change in Gail that he entered into the same commitment she had made. They fell in love with each other and in love with their children. In the thirteen years that have followed, they have helped hundreds of couples to build more fulfilling and lasting relationships. What was the principle Gail used? She began applying what the Bible calls *a quiet spirit* (1 Peter 3:4).

In 1 Peter 3:1–6, the apostle Peter describes four qualities God makes available to any woman. These qualities not only please God, but are highly motivating in changing a husband. One of these, the "quiet spirit" mentioned in verse 4, is the heart of inner beauty in a Christian woman.

Here's what Gail did. Like the holy women of old, she hoped in God and preferred her husband's needs to her own. She submitted herself to God, trusting Him to meet all her genuine needs (Phil. 4:19). She became anxious for nothing, but in *everything,* by praying and thanking God before she received from Him, she let God know her requests, and this *peace* began to *guard* her heart and mind in Christ Jesus (Phil. 4:6–7). She knew her needs would be well taken care of, so she was then free inside and able to focus on Mike's needs; that is, she had a quiet spirit—inner calmness. This calmness crowds out the fear so common in a wife's responses to her husband (1 Peter 3:6).

GENTLENESS

Gentleness is showing tender consideration for the feelings of another.

While I was visiting with a friend, we began talking about one of the most unusual couples either of us had ever known. What made them unique was that in their eighteen years of marriage they had never yelled at each other. I know this sounds hard to believe, and you might assume that the husband, Herb, is a Caspar Milquetoast kind of guy. Nothing could be further from the truth. Herb is an excellent athlete with engineering degrees and a very successful business. The fact that he has never yelled at Helen doesn't mean he hasn't yelled at anyone else.

The question is: How can a man who is as aggressive and self-motivated as Herb go eighteen years without yelling at his wife? As my friend and I thought about this, we looked at each other, smiled, and blurted out the answer in unison, "How could *anyone* ever yell at Helen?" Helen is a living picture of gentleness.

Have you ever noticed the difference between the way a father handles a newborn baby and the way he plays with a three-year-old? The first time I held my newborn son I was extremely careful and was so concerned I might hurt him that I handed him back to my wife rather quickly. By the time he was three, we were roughhousing almost nightly. Why was I less gentle with a three-year-old than I was with a newborn? When he was newborn, I was convinced that he was very fragile and that I needed to exercise the utmost care just to keep from hurting him.

The key motivation for gentleness is maintaining an awareness of the extreme fragility of other people's feelings. It was only natural for me to become less gentle physically with my son as he grew stronger. Unfortunately as time went on, I also became more calloused to my son's feelings because my busy schedule distracted my attention. Basically, I did what most of us do—I began to take Mike for granted. The more we take others for granted, the less gentle we tend to be in our relationship with them. We lose sight of their precious value and fragile inner person.

In other words, "The more we value something, the more gentle we will be in handling it." If I handed you a three-thousand-year-old, paper-thin Oriental vase worth $50,000 and asked you to take it to the bank, would you handle it any differently than if I gave you a 59¢ plastic vase and asked you to take it down the street?

Something happened to Mike that completely renewed my awareness of his priceless value and the fragility of his life. We were staying at a large motel, and I was swimming with my three children. While I was roughhousing with Kari and Greg, Mike was floating around in his Donald Duck inner tube. I turned around and saw the inner tube floating by itself in the deep end of the pool. Down in the water I saw Mike lying on the bottom of the pool—motionless, except for his soft, blond hair moving back and forth with the motion of the water. My heart was gripped with grief and fear as I dived down and brought him to the surface. After he recovered, I knew it would be a long time before I would take him for granted again. That was two years ago, and our closeness has continued to grow ever since.

There may be times when it is difficult for you to fully appreciate the priceless value of your husband, but the fact remains that he is a very special creation of God with needs, disappointments, hurts, and feelings just like anyone else. In the chapters that follow, we will be discussing specific ways you can express gentleness in your relationship with your husband and children.

UNSELFISH LOVE

Unselfish love is an action directed toward fulfilling another person's needs.

Nearly all of us enter marriage believing our love for our mate will never fade. Yet in the U.S. today, for every two marriages, there is one divorce. For too long we have accepted Hollywood's portrayal of love as the type of love for which to strive. It doesn't take long to discover that mere passion which revolves around sexual gratification is not sufficient in itself to establish a lasting relationship. Unfortunately, too many couples begin their marriages thinking this type of love is all they need.

There are at least three kinds of love, each totally unique. Of the three types of love—affection, passion, and genuine love—only the latter provides an adequate foundation for the other two types. If this type of love is missing, the relationship will most likely not be long-lasting. One of the most exciting virtues of genuine love is that God can build it within your character without the help of affectionate feelings (Gal. 5:22; Rom. 5:5). Before we look at genuine love, let's first consider the other two types of love.

FOR BETTER
Affection

The first type of love is recognizable when someone says, "I have fallen in love," or "I no longer love my husband." It's possible for people to "fall in love" and "fall out of love" because affection is based upon someone meeting *our* needs or living up to *our* expectations. As long as they meet our emotional, mental, and physical needs and live up to our expectations, we remain "in love" with them. When they cease to meet those expectations or fail to meet our needs, we can easily lose the affectionate feelings we have for them.

Passion

The second type of love is aptly described by the word "passion." This type of love is mainly centered around our need for sexual fulfillment. Like the first type of love, it is based upon our partner's ability to meet our needs—more specifically, our desire for romance and sex. This is the basis for most immature marriages—two young people longing for each other and getting married to guarantee that their mate will always be near to meet their needs. Passion is the weakest foundation for a marriage, as is evidenced by the high divorce rate among teenage marriages. A marriage must have passion to be fulfilling, but if passion is the thread that weaves the marriage together, the marriage has a much greater chance of unraveling.

Genuine Love

Genuine love is totally different from the first two types. Affection and passion make us aware of our own needs and cause us to look to others to meet those needs. Genuine love, as evidenced by Christ, searches for the needs of others and seeks opportunities to meet those needs (John 15:11–13). Simply stated, genuine love says, "I see your need; please allow me to meet it." Or as the apostle Paul defined it, "I submit myself to meeting your needs—your needs are my master" (Gal. 5:13–14). The focus of genuine love isn't receiving; it's giving. When a person receives genuine love from someone else, it can be one of the most powerfully motivating forces in his or her life.

I received a "D" in geometry the first time I took the course in high school. This qualified me for the "privilege" of taking the course a second time. I hated mathematics, and the second time around I was getting another "D." Midway through the course our teacher became ill and was replaced with a substitute. When the substitute walked into the classroom for the first time, we all gasped silently. His face was so disfigured that for the first week we looked out the window when we raised our hands to ask a question. By the end of the second week, his face was no longer a distraction because we felt the love he had for each one of us personally. He had begun to seek out what each one of us needed to improve our understanding of geometry. It was obvious to us that his highest concern was meeting our individual needs for learning the subject. He demonstrated his genuine love for me by staying after class on many occasions, doing everything he could to broaden my understanding of the subject. His eyes sparkled and his smile made him a very attractive person. His hidden beauty was what we all began to see. I was so motivated by his expression of love that my grade went from a "D" to an "A" in only six weeks. I went on to minor in mathematics in college as a result of this experience.

Genuine love doesn't necessarily spring from feelings. Its basis is primarily *a concern* for the welfare of another. Although the feelings of affection will follow, genuine love is initially an *action* directed toward fulfilling another person's needs.

The *first step* in developing genuine love for your husband is to begin valuing him as God does (John 3:16). It's committing yourself to care because he's worthwhile and because God cares a great deal about him. As you obey God's word in John 15:11–13, you receive the joy and peace Christ speaks of as a reward. God's plan is so terrific: you gain the life He promised, and you meet the deepest needs of your loved one at the same time.

In chapter 9 we will discuss the five basic needs of a man and how to meet them. But to genuinely love your husband, you have to go beyond those five basic needs and discover needs that are uniquely his. This *second step* involves using your creativity to meet his needs. This step is also discussed at length in chapter 9.

FOR PERSONAL REFLECTION

Developing these six inner-beauty qualities is a lifetime commitment. As these qualities become more and more a part of your character, your husband will find it much easier to learn *from you* what it takes to have a more fulfilling relationship. The remaining chapters will give you precise steps to help you begin motivating your husband to pursue a fulfilling and caring relationship. Many of these steps will produce visible results almost immediately. Others may take more time.

PART II

7

How To Increase Your Husband's Desire To Spend Quality Time With You

"And let the wife see to it that she respect (admire) her husband."

Ephesians 5:33

Before I married, there were certain types of girls that attracted me. They not only attracted me, but lots of other men as well. Finally, I decided to pinpoint the qualities they had that we all liked. By discussion and observation, I discovered at least six qualities they had in common. I believe that by taking these actions you can increase your husband's desire to set aside special moments with you: 1) Admire him; 2) Express a positive attitude on a consistent basis; 3) Focus more energy and concern on your inner beauty than on your outer appearance; 4) Compete with all his interests; 5) Use your unique feminine quality of gentleness; 6) Seek his opinion in your areas of interest.

ADMIRE HIM

Just as there are physical laws, such as the law of gravity, that govern our daily activities, so there are equally forceful and consistent relationship laws. One is the law of admiration. It reads: *People are attracted to those who admire them and repelled by those who belittle or look down on them.* Admiration is one of man's deepest and most important needs. That's probably why the Scriptures teach wives to admire their husbands (Eph. 5:33). The apostle Peter states that admiration can even motivate a husband spiritually (1 Peter 3:1–2).

The word *admire* (or *respect, honor*) in the Scriptures basically means "to attach high value to another." When the Word speaks of "fearing God," it simply means that God is to be most important to us—number one in our lives—and that is the beginning of wisdom (Prov. 9:10). Admire, respect, fear, and honor are similar in meaning, and all tell us to consider one another very worthwhile (Rom. 12:10).

The law of admiration is an extremely important part of this book, for it is the basis of all lasting, growing relationships. The vital part is that you don't have to like a person to admire him or her. Admiring someone is a choice, a decision, a commitment, an act of our will. It's telling ourselves, "God loves and values that person, and so can I."

Your husband might irritate you, belittle you, offend you, ignore you, or basically nauseate you, but admiration looks beyond what he does to who he is. It's unconditional.

Men tend to gravitate toward those who admire them.

The following quiz may pinpoint reasons why your husband does not want to spend as many hours with you as he does watching TV or pursuing other interests.

Quiz

1. *Have you ever shown more appreciation or admiration for other men than for your husband—perhaps for a pastor, a teacher, or another woman's husband? Even without his con-*

scious realization, your husband can be hurt by your esteem for other men. The questions, "Did you see Sarah and Jim at the party? Could you believe the ring he bought her?" may be telling your husband that Jim is more successful and generous than he is, that Jim treats Sarah better than your husband treats you. Or the statements, "I love being with Joan and Tom. Have you noticed how considerate he is?" may cause your husband to immediately assume that you believe he is not as considerate as Tom. Any statement of comparison, whether direct or implied, can tell your husband that you admire someone else more than him. Some men even avoid church because they feel they could never measure up to the minister their wives brag about on a weekly basis. Areas that are especially sensitive to a man include his job, his friends, his family heritage, and his intelligence. Be careful not to praise other men in his presence unless you are able to show even greater appreciation for your husband at the same time, or unless he is already secure in your admiration of him and your relationship is solid.

2. *Have you belittled or criticized your husband, his abilities, his character, or his activities?* This is especially destructive if done in front of his friends or children. Even the military—not generally known for its sensitivity to feelings—recognizes as the first basic principle of leadership, following basic training, that it is totally unacceptable to belittle a man's character or ability in front of others. I can think of nothing that demoralizes a man faster than criticism in front of his peers or his children.

3. *Have you ever had a tendency to exert pressure on him to do something until it gets done?* Nagging is another word for pressure from a wife that makes her husband feel incompetent and irresponsible. Rather than motivating him to fulfill his responsibility, it makes him want to ignore it. As you keep

nagging, he will seek other people who don't constantly remind him of his inadequacies. It's facial expressions and tone of voice that belittle and devalue a person.

4. *Do you find your trivial discussions turning into arguments?* He may view such discussions as an insult to his ability and intelligence, while you may be more realistically aware of the long-range problems caused by ignoring small things. But instead of challenging his unwillingness by arguing, look for indirect ways to expand his awareness of your world and get him to consider the full implications of what he is saying. (We'll go into more detail on this later in chapter 9.)

5. *Do you ever find yourself questioning his explanations of his behavior?* For example: If he calls you from the office to say he has to work late, do you ask him something like, "Do you really have to work late tonight?" With that one question, you imply you really don't trust his judgment. All he hears is your challenge of his judgment. No one likes to spend time with a "suspicious judge."

6. *Can you think of at least three things that you have complained about in the last week* (his schedule, his time with the kids, his lack of help around the house)? Complaining has the same effect as nagging. It repulses him.

7. *Have you ever compared your level of awareness to his?*
This lies at the heart of distinguishing maleness and femaleness. The apostle Peter calls a woman "the weaker vessel." The Greek word for *weaker* means "more sensitive" or more "fragile" (1 Peter 3:7; Rom. 14:1). Since women tend to be more aware of relationships and the nurturing aspects of life, it is reasonable to assume that your husband is not as aware as you are that something is missing between the two of you. If you expect him to desire the same level of intimacy as you, and if it offends you when he doesn't notice what seems obvious to you, your facial expressions and tone

of voice may communicate a judgmental and belittling attitude. Many women think their husbands lie awake at night thinking of offensive things to do to them. Well, it's just not true. Those things come natural for most men! If she doesn't understand that a man's basic drive is to conquer and find his identity in his vocation or activities, a woman can become hurt because she takes his attitude of indifference personally. She thinks he doesn't like her or the children. He interprets this anger or hurt as a put-down of him, especially if she says, "You should have known . . . or realized . . . or paid attention. . . ." The best way to begin helping a man indirectly is to accept him as a man and value him for what he is today and for what he will be through your loving and patient help. (Incidentally, we men need what a woman can give us for our own sake and well-being. We need to be more aware of feelings and what builds lasting relationships.)

PRACTICAL WAYS TO BEGIN EXPRESSING ADMIRATION FOR YOUR HUSBAND

In my discussions with various men, I have found that there are a variety of ways that their peers, secretaries, employers, and friends make them feel important. I have taken the ten most frequently suggested and have written a brief description on how you can apply them in your relationship.

1. *Begin to seek your husband's advice and opinions on decisions.* Consult him for reactions to furniture selection and arrangement, style and color of clothing, dinner options, etc. In doing this, try not to ask him open-ended questions like, "What do you want for dinner tonight?" Even though you have good intentions, you force him to think through something he may consider your responsibility. However, if you

ask, "What would you like for dinner—steak or spaghetti?" he appreciates your consideration. Don't overdo it though, for it might indicate to your husband that you are becoming too dependent and uncreative. Rather, maintain a balance by looking for special opportunities to seek his opinions and advice. As you carefully evaluate his ideas, he sees you consider him valuable.

2. *Make an effort to remember your husband's past requests and desires and begin to fulfill them when possible.* A close friend of mine told me his wife had done something that made him feel very special. Several weeks before he had remarked to her, "I wish I could watch just one football game from start to finish without getting interrupted." One day as he started to turn on a game, his wife came into the den, took both kids by the hand, and said, "Let's go up for a nap." After putting them to bed, she came in and said, "I'm going to go shopping now, and I hope you're able to enjoy this game without any interruptions. I've taken the phone off the hook so you won't be disturbed by any calls." What amazed him was that his wife remembered his comment made several weeks before and evidently had looked for the opportunity to do something about it. In appreciation, he began to work on some long overdue household projects.

Some facts about human relationships are as predictable as the laws of nature. As the example above proves: *no one can continually ignore considerate, loving actions.* If you make your husband feel special, you increase his desire to do the same for you. (However, if he takes advantage of you, use the idea of sharing your feelings in chapter 11.)

In the spaces below, list five requests your husband has made or implied. It could be a special event he wants to see or an activity he's been wanting to do; maybe a special meal you haven't made for a long time or one of his favorite desserts. As you begin to fulfill some of his past wishes, you may not receive any immediate encouragement from him. He may even say, "It's about time!" Rely on sheer willpower in difficult moments to see this project through, because the more you do it, the more fulfilling it will become for you.

1._____
2._____
3._____
4._____
5._____

3. *Look for occasional opportunities to draw attention to your husband's positive qualities when you're with other people.* For example: Praise him to your children, calling attention to his positive character qualities. If you are with friends and he says something worthwhile, tell him you think it makes a lot of sense and ask him to explain it further. Or, relate to friends or relatives a specific incident in the past week that highlights one of his positive qualities. For example: "John is so considerate of my feelings. The other day I hadn't said a word about how I felt, but he could tell I was down. He came over and put his arms around me. Then he told me he knew I was troubled and asked how he could help."

I can't begin to express how good I feel inside when people occasionally tell me something positive my wife has said about me. It makes me feel appreciated—I want to go home and put my arms around her as soon as I can!

4. *Make an effort to gain an appreciation for your husband's occupation, trying to understand how important he feels his job activities are.* Many men are frustrated with their jobs, feeling that no one really appreciates their worth or value, their talents and abilities. When you appreciate what your husband

does, you may become his *only* hope for achieving genuine self-worth. Until he really believes that he is worth something, he will have difficulty focusing his attention on the worth of others—including you.

Don't ever belittle his job or the importance of his activities on the job. Nothing destroys a man's self-esteem more than to hear his wife cutting down his efforts to support her. Though you may not criticize his efforts, you may belittle them by being ignorant of them. If you cannot accurately explain to someone else your husband's job responsibilities during his normal working day, you don't know enough about his job. Don't try to gain this knowledge from him at one sitting, but over a period of time begin to investigate by asking a few questions to gain a clearer understanding of how he spends his day, the types of projects he works on, and how his duties affect or support his fellow workers. (Be careful not to imply by the manner of your questioning that you think he loafs on the job.) Also, he may put down his job by little comments. When a man feels unimportant because of his job, it tears away at the very heart of his being. Help him discover the value of what he does.

5. *Carefully consider what your husband says without hasty negative reactions.* I am not promoting blind obedience, but rather open-minded listening. Often we demand *our* way on issues that could have been worked out in another way without creating major problems. If you have a tendency to react immediately when you hear his ideas, discipline yourself to withhold your reaction until his entire thought "sinks in" and you've had a chance to consider his idea fully. You will avoid unnecessary tension in your relationship, and he will enjoy being with you more. This is a good time to introduce the concept of submission. Submission is a beautiful biblical teaching that best illustrates genuine love. Unfortunately, it

has been misused until today the word is filled with distasteful connotations. Probably the most abuse has fallen from the hands of misguided husbands and "leaders" who have the mistaken idea that authority means "boss," decision-makers without regard for those under their authority.

Jesus said both in words and by example that anyone who wishes to be leader or ruler must first learn to be servant of all (Matt. 20:26–27). *Leaders are lovers.* They serve—submit to—and listen to those whom they would lead.

When a husband is loving his wife with understanding, gentleness, warmth, and communication, it is relatively easy for her to submit to him as a person. But even if your husband is not a loving person, you should still be practicing submission—love in action. It communicates to your husband that he is valuable and that his needs are more important than yours at the moment. (Equally important, husbands are to submit to their wives—more about this in his book—Ephesians 5:2).

A summary of this special biblical secret—*submission*

•I submit to God. I'll ask Him, and wait for Him, to meet all my needs (Ps. 62:1; Phil. 4:6-7,19).
•I realize how valuable I am to Christ because He gave His life for me (John 3:16).
•While waiting for my needs to be met through Christ, I'll attend to the needs of those around me. I'll forget about my needs because God's taking care of them (Eph. 3:19-20), and I'll focus on what I can do for others (John 15:11-12).

6. *Don't let two days pass without expressing appreciation for at least one thing your husband has said or done during those forty-eight hours.* Just a reminder. Don't forget how much nicer it is to be with people who make you feel special than with those who don't.

7. *Use your sensitivity to detect your husband's personal goals, and lend him your support as he pursues those goals.* His personal goals may involve advancement in his company, higher income, or special pastimes. A very successful businessman in Texas told me that his wife has always been supportive of his personal goals. Once she knew how important it was to him to be well-respected by others in his field, she helped him in a variety of ways to achieve this goal—through improving his taste in clothing, encouraging good personal grooming habits, etc. (He welcomed her help in this area because she didn't force her opinions upon him.) She encouraged him during times when he felt like quitting and praised him each time he attained any of his goals.

8. *Begin to admire your husband in nonverbal ways.* Studies of communication between husbands and wives have proven that words alone are responsible for only 7 percent of the total communication. Thirty-eight percent of marital communication is expressed through voice tone, and 55 percent through facial expressions and body movement. In other words, when you say something to your husband, the words themselves account for only 7 percent of the meaning. Take the phrase, "I love you." It can be said in a way that communicates, "Of course I love you; I pay the rent, don't I?" or it could be expressed in a way that says, "I adore you and couldn't live my life without you." Or, "I desperately need you to fulfill my needs right now." That's why I have heard so many wives responding to their husbands' "I love you" with, "You sure have

funny ways of showing it." Here are a few *nonverbal* ways to show your husband how important he is:

1. Be attentive to his concerns when he comes home.
2. Look as attractive as possible when he comes home.
3. Prepare appetizing meals.
4. Show interest and ask questions about his job, activities, problems, achievements.
5. Listen attentively by focusing your eyes on him.
6. Don't make him compete with the TV, the dishes, or even the children when he's trying to talk to you.

9. *Genuinely desire and seek your husband's forgiveness whenever you offend him.* Both men and women tend to avoid those who offend them. (One of the most common complaints children make about their parents is that parents never admit they are wrong.) The key to "wiping the slate clean" with your husband is not saying, "I'm sorry." That's a phrase even children exploit to avoid a spanking. When we have been offended by someone, we usually don't want to hear a glib "I'm sorry." We want to know that the person realizes he or she was wrong and that he or she hurt us. I believe there are a lot of "wrong ways" to ask forgiveness. They are wrong because they do not bring us into harmony with the person whom we have offended and they may not communicate the person's value to us. For example, avoid saying:

1. I'm sorry *if* I was wrong; I *hope* I didn't hurt you.
2. I'm sorry I did that; I really didn't mean it to hurt you.
3. I'm sorry I said what I said, but you were wrong too.
4. I'm sorry. Next time I'll try to be more careful.

With apologies like these, your husband will feel you are not accepting full responsibility for your action. You are either minimizing the degree to which you hurt him or you are minimizing your role in inflicting the hurt. As a result, he may sense that your apology is insincere. Though he may say, "I forgive you," he will be saying to himself, "She really isn't sorry at all. She's just trying to get rid of her guilt."

One of the best ways I have found to ask forgiveness is, unfortunately, the hardest and the least creative. All it requires is that you go to your husband, look into his eyes, and say, "I was wrong in what I said or did. Can you forgive me?" Two things will happen when you ask for forgiveness in this way. First, your husband will desire to restore the relationship and will be more prepared to forgive you; and second, it is likely to exert pressure on him to ask for forgiveness in the future for the ways he has offended you. As a side benefit, it makes him feel important—you are telling him indirectly that you care for him enough not to leave him with hurt feelings.

EXPRESS A POSITIVE ATTITUDE ON A CONSISTENT BASIS

While in college I dated a lot of different girls. Eventually I met a girl who had a particular *quality* that attracted me like a magnet. Even though I was still dating others, I called her almost every day, spending an hour or two on the phone with her.

The magnetic quality that kept me racing for the telephone was this girl's positive attitude. She was always so much fun to talk to, never doing or even saying negative things. Instead, she was always encouraging and positive. Four years later we married, and today, after fourteen years of marriage, her positive outlook on life continues to be a tremendous source of joy and strength. She uses her alertness and awareness to look beyond surface issues, and she often sees positive benefits in situations that appear dark and hopeless to me.

If you want your husband to yearn for quality time with you, then it is essential that you develop and express a positive attitude. You might say, "But if you knew my husband . . . if you knew what I'm going through . . . it's just impossible for me to develop a positive attitude." Just ask yourself these questions:

- How do I act around our dinner guests when I have a headache?
- How do I act when I'm in a hurry at the grocery store and run into a friend with problems?

We usually find it easy, or at least necessary, to have a positive attitude around our friends and associates. Don't you agree that our mates deserve the same consideration?

When your husband comes home from work, the worst thing you can do is greet him with a negative comment about something he forgot to do or some disaster you encountered during the day.

I am not saying that you shouldn't talk about negative things. But I am stressing that there is a right way and a right time to talk about them. Wait until he's had a chance to rest or until the house is quiet after the kids have gone to bed. If a negative situation is so important that you have to confront him with it as soon as he comes home—then use the salt principle (chapter 5). Negative greetings should be the exception, not the rule. Your husband's homecoming should be as peaceful as possible (unless your son has just been arrested or the IRS wants to audit your tax return immediately).

Have you ever wondered why people gravitate toward the negative rather than the positive? The answer is simple. Our very natures tend to be negative. It seems no matter how good a situation is, we are able to find something negative in it. For example, which of the following sets of numbers attract your attention most quickly?

$$2+2=4 \quad 5+6=11 \quad 7+8=17 \quad 8+8=16$$
$$9+11=20$$

Which of the five words below attracts your attention most quickly?

read   love   crisp   develp   smart

Notice that your eyes automatically dwell on the incorrect problem ($7 + 8 = 17$) and the misspelled word (develp).

We all tend to notice the negative. So most of the information in our newspapers and on television broadcasts revolves around negative issues. And that's why we all enjoy a "juicy tidbit" of gossip.

Negative thinking, especially about ourselves, is a major cause for an overall negative outlook on life. What we say to ourselves about a problem actually has stronger effect on our feelings than the problem itself. We all tend to bombard ourselves with short sentences like: "I'm no good." "I'm a failure." "I can't do anything right." "He doesn't like me." "This guy is driving me crazy." "I'm coming unglued." "You're blowing my mind." "I'm sick and tired of this." All these short, negative statements focusing on the bad side of things produce a negative attitude. The ultimate result of a lifetime of negative thinking is frustration, despair, and depression. In fact, a psychiatrist recently told me he believes two words alone can keep a person in a mental institution: "If only. . . ."

It's very important to understand that much of depression and discouragement is directly related to negative thoughts. If at 9:00 A.M. we start thinking, "I'm no good," or "I'm a failure," or "He doesn't like me," we'll be depressed by 11:00 A.M.

Our feelings *follow* our thinking and/or actions. If our thinking and actions are positive, then our feelings *will be* positive in a matter of hours (The Scriptures teach that as a person "thinks within himself, so is he" [Prov. 23:7]).

GAINING A POSITIVE ATTITUDE

I once counseled a young wife who had been sexually attacked when she was a young girl. I could see by the expression on her face that she was still discouraged and distressed about the incident and embarrassed to talk about it. Feeling she had been cheated in life, she was somewhat resentful that God had allowed such a horrible thing to happen. Still unable to eliminate her deep feeling of shame over the situation, she began to discuss how she felt about it now as an adult.

I began by telling her she would never be free from the resentment, shame, and negative attitude resulting from her experience unless she could first see the benefits which resulted from the attack. She looked at me like I was crazy when she asked, "What benefits?"

"I'm going to ask you a very difficult question based on two Scriptures—1 Thessalonians 5:18 and Romans 8:28. Do you think that right now you could thank God that this *happened* to you?"

"You've got to be kidding," she said. "I could never thank God. The only thing I could ever be thankful for is that I didn't become mentally ill because of the attack. I'm thankful for that."

"I'm not asking you to be 'thankful' that it was a terrible experience. I'm just asking you to be willing to say, 'Thank You, God, for that attack because I know You can turn it into good. I just can't see the good now' " (Isa. 61:3; Rom. 8:28).

She didn't think she could do that, which was understandable. However, I told her she could work through her feelings, and then I asked her if she would like my help. She responded, "By all means."

"First, let's look at your dating life before you got married. Did you ever let anyone take advantage of you sexually when you were dating?"

She replied, "Absolutely not! When that man did that to me, I said no other man would *ever* take advantage of me again."

"So in other words, because that happened to you as a child, you never got involved in any immorality in high school or college. Consequently, you have been spared the hurts that can come from an illicit relationship. It may have even saved you from the consequences of pregnancy before marriage. In essence, that man gave you a vaccination that may have saved you from worse problems," I said.

"Yeah, I never thought of it like that, but that's exactly what happened," she replied.

"Now I'm going to show you the most important thing of all. You received a gift at the very time the attack took place. Do you know what I'm referring to?"

"No, what is it?"

"You received a priceless quality that will enable you to better love others in a genuine way. That is, *greater sensitivity.* How alert are you to your children's needs and your husband's needs?"

"Very alert!"

"I can believe that. It's only natural that when something terrible happens to us, we become even more aware of and sensitive to the sufferings of those around us. Awareness and sensitivity then become the basis for genuine love—being able to detect another person's need and having the motivation to meet that need in the most effective way."

I continued by asking what kind of man she had married. Was he calloused or gentle? She said her husband was a very loving, tender, gentle man. She considered him a wonderful husband. It became increasingly obvious to both of us that because she had been abused by a man, she had become more aware of her need for a gentle and compassionate husband. She realized how the experience had "sensitized" her to the type of husband she really needed.

By the time she left my office, she had all the reasons she needed to thank God for her past. After being in bondage to negative feelings for years, she was set free simply by thinking through the positive factors involved.

The first step in gaining a positive attitude is to discover the benefits of the negative situation. (Incidentally, I haven't heard of a situation yet that lacked positive benefits.) It often seems the more tragic the situation, the greater the positive consequences. I am not saying that the beneficial outcome of a negative situation justifies the situation. Absolutely not. I am saying that as we recognize the *positive side* of a negative situation, we can be liberated from the chains that tie us to guilt, resentment, despair, and any other negative feeling which has held us captive.

With this principle, I must include two cautions: First, I am not providing an excuse to do something wrong, with the rationalization that something good will come of it. I believe that such reasoning is shallow and perverted in that the wrongdoer is always the loser (Luke 17:1–2). Second, people who are suffering from tragedy don't need flippant statements such as, "I know you can find some good in this if you really try." So first be sensitive to their emotions and their immediate needs for *comfort*. When the time is right, after empathic comfort has been extended graciously and gently, then you can begin to help them see the benefits of their problems.

The more you discover the inherent benefits of *your own* problems, the more positive your attitude will become. As a result, your husband will desire to spend more time with you.

FOCUS MORE ENERGY AND CONCERN ON YOUR INNER BEAUTY THAN ON YOUR OUTER APPEARANCE

It's obvious that women and men alike usually spend more time and energy trying to groom their exteriors than strengthen their interiors. A woman should do everything she can to make herself physically attractive to her husband.

However, outer beauty will only attract a man's *eye*, but inner beauty will keep his *heart* (1 Peter 3:1–6).

We discussed at length in chapter 6 several inner beauty qualities that can melt almost any man's heart: courage, persistence, gratefulness, calmness, gentleness, and genuine love. For your convenience, I will review in capsule form the working definitions of each of these qualities:

1. Courage:	The inner *commitment* to pursue a worthwhile goal without giving up hope.
2. Persistence:	*Continuing* to pursue a goal until it is achieved.
3. Gratefulness:	A sincere *appreciation* for the benefits received from others.
4. Calmness:	An inner *peace* that allows you to respond quietly to a stressful situation without fear.
5. Gentleness:	Showing *tender consideration* for the feelings of another.
6. Genuine Love:	Meeting the *needs* of another, prior to your own personal needs being met.

COMPETE WITH ALL HIS INTERESTS

Every wife needs to ask herself these searching questions:

"Why would my husband want to spend more time with me?"
"Would *I* even want to spend more time with me?"
"What can I do to make myself more attractive?"

FOR BETTER

"What can I do to become more attractive to my husband?"

"How can I become more attractive than his other interests?"

The first step in competing for your husband's attention is to make yourself more interesting and attractive. For example, one woman deeply resented being second to other people or her husband's job. After harboring this resentment for several years, she finally began to understand WHY he preferred the company of others. During one particularly miserable trip, she had been moody and grouchy most of the time because her husband had been busy with other people. After giving it a great deal of thought, *she realized* that her husband didn't want to spend time with her because the things she enjoyed simply were not interesting to him (visiting dress shops, jewelry stores, etc.). After that wretched vacation, she determined to make herself more appealing and fascinating.

So while her husband took an extended trip, she decided to make some drastic personal changes. She lost weight, changed her hairstyle, and purchased a few fashionable outfits. But *most important*, she began to change some of her attitudes. She made a special effort to work on qualities of inner beauty. When her husband sighted her waiting at the airport after his trip, he said he honestly wondered, *Who's the beautiful blonde in the sunglasses?* He couldn't believe the difference. He not only began to spend more time with his "new" wife, but he became more alert in areas where he had never shown any sensitivity whatsoever.

When your husband comes home from work each night, how do you look? Is your hair fixed up? How about your clothes? When he goes into the kitchen or dining room to eat dinner, is the table setting attractive and neat? Do you

102

fix some of the food he really likes the way he likes it? In every area of your life, discover how you can be so attractive that he would rather be with you than anyone or anything else. (Remember, this effort is not just for your benefit; it is for his, too, in all his relationships, especially with your children.)

Giving admiration or respect is the second step in competing for your husband. He hungers for sincere admiration and respect, and he will gravitate toward those who admire him, his personality, or his talents. This need for admiration motivates men to spend time on committees, run for political offices, and enter various competitive sports. In fact, many men compete in strenuous events just to receive a trophy—the tangible symbol of accomplishment.

The third step in competing for his attention requires that you show more interest in his life than anyone else does—more than his friends, his colleagues at the office, or any of his associates. Imagine the impact on your relationship if you gave your husband a daily dose of genuine interest. He would probably leave friends or work early to get home to you. Don't laugh! It's possible.

I remember a young woman who came to my office emotionally broken and distraught after her husband had told her he had been seeing another woman. He was planning to leave, although he would stay until their baby was born. When he told her, she became hysterical. She said, "As I thought about losing him, I was so upset that my very reaction repulsed him. I'm sure that even my facial expression communicated an intolerable ugliness to him."

The remaining weeks would be a precious commodity. I told her to use every available moment to compete with the other woman. She did just that. She recalled some of his favorite meals and fixed them. She jotted down his interests and began centering her conversations around them. Giving attention to her appearance, she tried to look her best each evening when he came home from work. And above all, she never demanded that he remain at home, although she knew he was probably going out to be with the other woman. She became more fluent in her admiration of him and began to do little things she thought would mean a lot to him. At first he resisted her efforts, telling her she was wasting her time. *But she persisted.*

Within three months, her husband had quit seeing the other woman because of the changes he saw in his wife. He said he saw a beauty in her he had never seen before, the inner beauty she had worked so hard to develop. Her strong interest in her husband, plus sensitivity to his needs, had overcome anything the other woman could offer.

USE YOUR UNIQUE FEMININE QUALITY OF GENTLENESS

Have you ever been driven to he point of losing control? Screaming, swearing, breaking things in outbursts of anger *can* result from the need for a deeper relationship with your husband. As he fails to meet this need, you become so frustrated that you explode from time to time. These explosions may rearrange the furniture, but they do nothing to change his behavior.

I'm sure you're keenly aware of your husband's deficiencies; however, it is of upmost importance that you refrain from confronting him with them in anger. As we've said before, a man has a tendency to fight his conscience; and if you become his conscience, he'll either fight you or flee you.

Whichever route he takes, you've lost your goal of spending more time with him.

You need to tell your husband how important it is to spend time together. But tell him in a gentle, loving way at the right time. Explain to your husband some of the important occasions you'd like to spend with him—anniversaries, birthdays, holidays, and other times that are special to you. *Then find out what times he would like to share with you.*

It's also important to discuss the types of activities you would like to do together. That is, times you'd like to be alone with him or out with friends, with your children or without your children. (Ever tried an overnight campout with him alone? Just remember—when the sun goes down, a couple of hours remain when some great uninterrupted communication can take place.) Let him know that when he spends time with you, he's really doing himself a favor. Explain that the closer your relationship becomes, the more responsive you'll be in meeting his physical needs. Explain, too, that as your relationship grows you'll gain a stronger desire to do things especially for him—fixing special meals, dressing the way he prefers, attending sporting events with him. I believe one of the best ways you can recognize and meet your husband's unique needs is to develop and maintain open communication through a growing relationship with him.

I often wondered what provoked some women to eat their way to obesity. Would you believe, one reason is a lack of communication? It's true. I found that their compulsive eating is often directly related to apathetic husbands. Just the feeling of an incomplete relationship can cause some women to turn to the refrigerator for comfort. As a woman gains weight, her husband's rejection, combined with her feelings of guilt, puts even more pressure on her. Frustrated and nervous, she becomes more compulsive in her eating. The only way she can get off this vicious treadmill is to communicate to her husband—*in a gentle way*—that she needs his understanding and acceptance.

By explaining your feelings and needs gently, lovingly and calmly, it becomes obvious that you're not being selfish in asking him to spend quality time with you. A lack of time with him affects you and your relationship with him.

SEEK HIS OPINION IN YOUR AREAS OF INTEREST

One of Bonney's majors in college was home economics, including training in interior design. She is an extremely creative woman and needs no help from her husband in decorating a room. Whether choosing wallpaper or carpeting, picking lamps or arranging furniture, she has the ability to create just the feeling she wants in a room through tasteful choice of decor. Steve is aware of his wife's talent; he realizes Bonney needs no help when it comes to furnishing their home. But on many occasions she has made him feel needed and appreciated by seeking his opinion on carpet samples, fabrics, etc. She never belittles his taste, and as a result, he tells me he always looks forward to doing things with her.

Many men appreciate it when their wives ask for help. My wife can always get me to join her simply by starting a repair project. If she asks me to do it, usually I'm not interested. But as soon as I see her struggling with some repair, I jump in and we fix it *together.* I really enjoy it when she gently asks for my help without expectation and then expresses gratefulness for my time. You may think, *Why should a woman even have to do all that to get her husband to spend time with her?*

OR FOR BEST

It just doesn't seem fair! I agree with you. But the fact of the matter is that men are buffalos and women are butterflies. Your buffalo may never gain butterfly sensitivity unless you provide the motivation.

However, you should beware of several pitfalls at this point. First, when you recruit his help, don't criticize him for doing the job worse than you would have done it yourself. Criticizing his work is the fastest way to discourage him from working side-by-side with you again. If he does something which fails to meet your standards, bite your tongue.

Second, if he gives an answer you don't like when you've asked his advice, don't start an argument. You can easily avoid arguments by offering him choices you know you can live with when you ask for his advice. For example: If you want his opinion of wallpaper, don't give him a wallpaper book with five hundred samples. Narrow the field to several different patterns with which you are satisfied. Then ask him to decide which of those patterns he prefers. If he doesn't like any of them, go back and study the books and then bring him several more choices.

My last caution is: Be selective about asking for his help, and never embarrass him.

Immediately after graduate school, our income was much too low for us to buy ready-made draperies for our living room. So Norma made them at home, with my assistance. After a crash course on how to use a sewing machine, I worked with Norma almost from start to finish on those curtains. They weren't the best-looking in the world, but we enjoyed our joint accomplishment. And I gained a greater appreciation for all the little things that go into sewing and making drapes.

Sounds good, right? Wrong!

I'll never forget the day that I was driving down the road

with the chairman of the education board, on which I served, and he said, "I was talking with your wife, and she told me that you helped her make some curtains." He gave me a funny look and asked, "Do you really enjoy sewing?" I was so embarrassed that I vowed never again to help my wife in any area which could be misconstrued by others. If she had said something like, "I really appreciated my husband's help in designing our curtains," it wouldn't have been as embarrassing. But I felt ridiculous when people knew I actually sat at her sewing machine and made curtains. It was even worse to be asked if I really enjoyed sewing. Now that I'm more "mature," I wouldn't mind admitting something like this. But at my young age my ego just couldn't take it.

The six motivating factors discussed in this chapter really work. It would be impossible for anyone to develop and apply all of these overnight, but in time, you will have countless opportunities to use each one. When you do, you will find your husband gravitating toward your admiration and respect; your positive attitude will be a source of encouragement and strength that he'll begin to depend on more and more; and everyone will gain by your commitment to him.

FOR PERSONAL REFLECTION
1. Why would a husband believe the Word without a word being spoken by his wife? 1 Peter 3:2.
2. How does Romans 12:10 apply to the word *submission*. Carefully define this word for your own relationship.

8

How To Gain
Your Husband's
Undivided Attention
On a Consistent Basis

"An excellent wife, who can find? For her worth is far above jewels."

Proverbs 31:10

On a recent flight to Los Angeles the pilot announced that a world-famous cheerleading squad was aboard and would be strolling the aisles singing "Happy Birthday" to anyone who had a birthday that month. When they finished singing, I asked if I could interview the married members of the group for a book I was writing. They graciously consented, and I had the opportunity to spend more than an hour with two of them. One had been married for a year; the other had been married for three years. Both were articulate, intelligent, and physically attractive.

I started our interview by asking them what was the greatest single disappointment in their marriages. Their answers? Each said it was nearly impossible to get her husband's undivided attention unless he had ulterior motives.

I wasn't surprised that they gave the same answer. I have heard it from hundreds of women, young and old, attractive and unattractive. The "Inattentive husband" seems to be a universal complaint among women. Both of the cheerleaders said they had given up any hope of seeing a change in their marriages. They had slumped into what society says is "only natural."

It *isn't* "only natural," and it *can* be changed! No matter what your situation is, there are at least four ways to gain your husband's consistent, undivided attention. Both of the NFL cheerleaders were excited to learn how to make their husbands eager to listen, and you, too, can be encouraged by the changes possible through use of the following principles.

LIGHT UP

Something about my father attracted me like a magnet. When school was out, many times I would rush to his hardware store instead of going out with my friends. What drew me to my father? Why did I prefer a visit with him over some of my favorite activities? As soon as I set foot in his store, it seemed as if his whole personality lit up. His eyes sparkled, his smile gleamed, and his facial expressions immediately conveyed how glad he was to see me. I almost expected him to announce, "Look, everybody, my son is here." I loved it. Although I didn't realize it at the time, those tremendously powerful nonverbal expressions were the magnets that drew me to him.

Ninety-three percent of our communication is nonverbal. Your husband can be attracted or repelled most often, then, by your nonverbal behavior. If he comes home from work to a worn facial expressoin that says, "Oh, brother, look who's home—Mr. Gripe," or "It's only you," then of course he will be repulsed. Whenever you see him, you've got to "light up" with enthusiasm, especially in your facial expressions and tone of voice. That light comes from the inner knowledge that he's valuable. Norma shows that sparkle whenever I walk in the door, and consequently, I want to spend time talking to her and listening to her. If she "lights up" when a particular subject is mentioned, she increases my desire to talk about that subject; as a result, I enjoy listening to her, her opinions, and her needs.

As a husband "sees" your sincere expressions of his worth, he will be drawn to you (1 Peter 3:1–2).

The students in a psychology class picked up on the powerful effect of "lighting up" when someone is talking. They met after class without the professor and decided to try an experiment. Every time the professor walked close to the room heater (a radiator) they agreed to appear more attentive—sit up straight, liven their facial expressions, take notes more diligently—to look as interested as possible without being too obvious. Each time their professor walked away from the radiator, their interest in his lectures would dwindle noticeably—they would look at each other with bored expressions, slouch in their chairs. Their experiment proved the "lighting up" principle. Within a few weeks the professor was giving his entire lecture while seated on the radiator.

While I was in college, I decided to try a similar experiment of my own. I asked my ten-year-old niece, Debby, to make up one hundred sentences using any one of the following pronouns: he, she, we, they, it, or I. I had predetermined that every time she used the pronoun "he," I would make encouraging movements with my body or positive expressions with my face and tone of voice. Each time she used other pronouns, I would sit back in my chair, look bored, and mumble in an indifferent tone of voice.

By the time we reached the fiftieth sentence, Debby was

using the pronoun "he" in every sentence and continued to do so until we finished. Unaware of what I had been doing, Debby said she thought I had been checking on her sentence structure. She was unaware of her frequent usage of "he." Since then I have used the "light up" technique to demonstrate that I am genuinely interested in what others are saying. I've also found that my positive nonverbal communication increases others' interest in what I say.

I encourage you to use this technique to show your husband how *important* he is. It's an invaluable way to build a more loving relationship.

LEARN MORE ABOUT HIS INTERESTS AND VOCATION

Many men allow their hobbies to be a consuming passion. They live, breathe, eat, and sleep their hobby or vocation. One woman told me she wanted to build a deeper relationship with her outdoorsman husband, but she knew nothing about hunting and fishing. She decided the only way to become knowledgeable about her husband's interest was to take up hunting and fishing herself. She actually had no desire to hunt and fish, but she *did* desire a deeper relationship with her husband.

First, she asked him to teach her how to shoot a gun. They spent hours at the firing range as she endured the necessary practice. Next on the agenda—a fishing trip, which proved frustrating due to her lack of skill. So, she practiced casting in their backyard and found that her enjoyment increased as her skill improved. In the early weeks of "training" she became discouraged and thought the whole idea a waste of time. But she persisted. Now an excellent marksman, she enjoys hunting and fishing with her husband. Not only have their shared experiences drawn them closer, but more important, they have developed a common interest which they both enjoy discussing. It's easy for her to gain his undivided attention simply by beginning a conversation about hunting or fishing and then moving to other subjects.

If you feel your husband lacks the patience necessary to teach you one of his hobbies, don't let it stop you from learning. Simply seek another source of instruction. Professional instruction is readily available in almost every sport or interest. Try the lessons to see if you've got what it takes to "stick it out," and then surprise him after you've gained some proficiency. If you tell him about your intentions before you start, he might not believe that you will follow through. He might even discourage you from trying.

Nearly every man is interested in some type of sport—either as a spectator or a participant. Whatever sport your husband enjoys watching on TV, try to develop an appreciation for it. At first it may bore you to tears, but as you learn the rules, techniques, etc., you will enjoy the sport more. Pay as much attention to what's going on as your husband does, otherwise you will be distracting. If he is watching a football game and you decide to do a little knitting on the side, chances are you'll drive him up the wall. As far as he's concerned, interest without attentiveness is really no interest at all. (Incidentally, the more you find out about the personal lives and families of professional athletes, the more your interest will increase.)

As we mentioned in chapter 7, every man needs to feel admired. Because he spends the largest part of his day at work, his identity becomes linked to his job, just as your identity is linked to your home and family or your own vocation. If you aren't excited about his work, it's nearly impossible for him to believe that you admire him for anything. Consequently, it is extremely important that you learn enough about his responsibilities to express a genuine interest in them. You can't learn everything about his work overnight. Take your time about it.

One woman told me she was repulsed by her husband's occupation as a trucker. She categorized all truckers as morally loose, rough, crude, and dirty. Although she never *said* anything negative to him, her nonverbal behavior got the message across. And slowly but surely, her husband lost interest in spending time with her.

I encouraged her to take a closer look at the trucking industry and the tremendous services it provides for our society. I reminded her that nearly everything she owned was delivered via truck . . . virtually every other industry is dependent on the trucking industry . . . a truckers' strike practically paralyzes our society. I told her about the numerous times my family has been assisted by truckers willing to stop and help when our cars were broken down on the highway.

I suggested that she begin to ask her husband about the different types of goods he delivers, the towns he goes through, the people he meets, and the discouraging problems he faces. Within a month she had a new appreciation for the value as well as the difficulty of his job.

USE THE SALT PRINCIPLE TO GAIN YOUR HUSBAND'S ATTENTION

In chapter 5 we discussed the salt principle and how it works. If you are still somewhat unsure about this principle, it might be good to review that chapter before you read further.

The salt principle is undoubtedly the most effective way to gain your husband's undivided attention. Although learning to use this technique does take some practice, once you've mastered it, you will invariably gain his full attention—even if he knows what you're doing. Remember to use this technique with a loving, gentle, kind attitude. If your attitude or tone of voice reflects pride or cockiness, your husband will only resent your attempt to arouse his curiosity. He will consider it a weapon, especially if you use it to create curiosity and then refuse to fulfill it with something like, "Well, I'll just tell you later when you have a better attitude!" I can't think of a better way to immunize your husband against the effectiveness of the salt principle.

With the right attitude, the salt principle is so powerful that it works even when the listener is in a hurry or under pressure. You don't have to wait until your husband is free from tension and deadlines to stimulate his curiosity. Just give it all you've got with salty questions, pleasant facial expressions, and a gentle tone of voice.

TEACH YOUR HUSBAND TO LISTEN TO YOU

By now I hope I've made one point clear: *most* men do not understand women. Since you know your needs better than anyone else, you can be your husband's most effective teacher. He needs to learn from you *why* it's important to listen to you and *how* to listen.

First, explain why it's important to you that he spend time listening with his undivided attention. (The woman called "virtuous" [also, "excellent"] in Proverbs 31:10 was so called because she had convictions and influence. Convictions bring influence. When you're sold on something, like the im-

115

portance of a better relationship, it will show through your facial expressions.) Let him know that when he doesn't listen to you attentively, it makes you feel unimportant and unappreciated. Explain that this, in turn, decreases your desire to meet his needs. Make it clear, however, that the opposite is also true. When he consistently listens to you with attentiveness, you feel more important and have a much stronger desire to meet his needs with greater creativity. You may have to tell him these things repeatedly before they sink in. But each time the opportunity arises, you have another chance to stimulate his curiosity.

In addition to explaining *why* you need his undivided attention, you must show him *how* to give it. Discuss the nonverbal means of communication with him. As he learns to understand your feelings by looking at your eyes and facial expressions, your communication and your relationship will deepen. Gently remind him that his partial listening doesn't do any good, that you don't want to compete with work, sports, and TV.

Be careful not to let your times of communication deteriorate into arguments. Use your sensitivity to learn how to sidestep issues, words, or mannerisms that ignite an argument. Some women concede that the only way they get their husband's undivided attention is to start an argument. Unfortunately, that's not the type of undivided attention which builds a healthy relationship. Let your communication be as encouraging and delightful as possible.

Learning to gain your husband's undivided attention on a consistent basis will be a major undertaking. However, gaining his attention is not an end in itself. It is a means to develop several beautiful facets to your relationship. One of those facets, helping your husband become aware of your emotional and romantic needs, will be discussed in detail in chapter 9.

FOR PERSONAL REFLECTION

Why was the Proverbs 31 woman so honored by her husband? Proverbs 31:10–31. List ten inner qualities of this woman.

9

How To Increase Your Husband's Sensitivity To Your Emotional Needs And Desires

"An excellent wife is the crown of her husband, but she who shames him is as rottenness in his bones."

Proverbs 12:4

Most women have a short, simple definition for romance and emotional tenderness—"the little things." Ever tried to explain to your husband what those "little things" are? One woman told me, "My husband thinks he's doing me a big favor by buying me a new toaster. But for some reason, that just doesn't mean as much as it would for him to greet me early in the morning by taking my hand or kissing me on the cheek to tell me that he thinks I'm really special."

A woman can become so much a part of her children, her home, and her daily routine that she often loses her identity as an individual. Consequently, she feels a deep need to be singled out, loved individually. No woman wants to be viewed merely as the wife, the other laborer, the cook, the cleaning lady, the mother, the ironing service, the laundress, or the family chauffeur. It's not enough that her family show deep appreciation for the role she fulfills. She has a need for her husband to draw her out of that demanding role and love

119

her for *who she is* rather than for *what she does*. Once he gains a sensitivity to her emotional needs and desires, he can begin to fulfill them with creative actions that women call, "the little things." (For your husband's benefit, I discuss this in greater detail in the book *If Only He Knew*.)

You can provide your husband with the motivation and the knowledge necessary to meet your needs by cultivating three new skills: 1) sow seeds of love; 2) explain your unique needs and desires; 3) express your gratefulness without expectation.

SOW SEEDS OF LOVE

We reap what we sow (Gal. 6:7). You've heard it a hundred times, but it's just as true now as it was thousands of years ago. If you're rude and contentious, people will respond to you in the same way. Conversely, if you're thoughtful and gentle, it's difficult for others to respond with anything less. As you detect your husband's needs and make special efforts to fulfill them, eventually he will notice your efforts and appreciate you. Out of his appreciation will grow a desire to enrich your relationship. If you start by sowing seeds of love and care for your husband, soon you'll be reaping his love and appreciation.

Discover your husband's distinctive needs.

Some women presume to know all of their husband's needs without even asking them. But I have never met a man who could say his mate knew *all* about *all* of him.

It's always fun to meet the wife who thinks she has her mate completely figured out. In total confidence she says, "I know exactly why he does that," or "I know him inside out." But all I have to do is ask a few questions to reveal that the "know-it-all" partner knows a lot less about her spouse than she thought. Many couples, thinking they know each other intimately, have actually lived on a superficial level for years. Unfortunately, marriages of this type are the norm rather than the exception.

Get past the superficial by discovering the individuality of your mate. Although your husband is similar to other men, he is totally unique . . . one of a kind. He is different in temperament, personality, childhood, adolescence, family relationships, heritage, talents, goals, aspirations, successes, failures, frustrations, and disappointments. You must abandon the idea that he's just like all other men, another common, everyday, average guy. Finding out *who he is* and *what he feels* can be one of the most stimulating and rewarding investments of your life. Sometime you might ask him, "What really fulfills you as a man?" Listen carefully as he shares some of his deepest feelings. Make a list of the things he shares some of his deepest feelings. Make a list of the things he shares, and demonstrate your interest in them by talking about them from time to time. Try to discover the things that hurt and disappoint him. In other words, begin to really know your man.

Next, consider some general needs common to men. As you think about them, keep in mind that you may have to tailor each one to fit your own husband.

NEEDS COMMON TO MEN

Men need to be loved.

*   *   *

Obviously, if your husband preferred living alone, you wouldn't be married to him right now. Every man needs to know that someone, somewhere in the world cares about him. He needs to know he has a committed, intimate friend who will like him no matter what he does. Just like you, he needs the security of genuine love. That's why the older women are to teach the younger women to love their husbands (Titus 2:4).

Genuine love is far more than a feeling; it's the kind of love that last a lifetime. It means a commitment to care for the loved one unconditionally. It says, "I'm committed to you no matter how you treat me or what happens." Genuine love does not depend upon emotions or circumstances. It takes full advantage of the present to bring meaning and joy to the lives of others. If your marriage is to become all that you long for, you must *begin today*, right now, to develop the unconditional love which forms the foundation of a fulfilling marriage.

As you begin to develop genuine love, it's quite possible that you will lack romantic feelings. Don't be discouraged. I guarantee that if you persist in expressing genuine love in actions and words because he's worthwhile, eventually the feelings will follow. And the romantic love you once shared with your husband will return. The notion that genuine love is something you feel at all times is a drastic misconception. Feelings are changeable—they can come and go. But love is an unchanging commitment. Your husband needs to sense your unconditional acceptance of him as a person—that you value his opinions no matter how he phrases them; that you are concerned for him no matter how unnerving his habits. He needs to know that you carefully, thoughtfully listen to what he says and that you consider his words and actions worthwhile.

Men need to be admired.

Men will do almost anything to gain the admiration of others. They will literally search for someone to love and respect them—and you can be that someone to your husband by letting him know you're interested in him, that you desire to know what's behind his decisions and the direction he's going.

Take advantage of the variety of ways to express genuine admiration. When he's down, don't react with disgust. Maintain respect for him as you comfort him quietly and gently. When you've hurt his feelings, admit you were wrong and ask for his forgiveness. When he shares an idea with you that doesn't sit right, don't come unglued. He needs the confidence and security of knowing that you won't react negatively to his ideas. Give him the same confidence that you have in the chair you're sitting in—a confidence that allows him to rest and relax with you. (If you need more ideas on how to admire your husband, refer to chapter 7.)

Men need to be understood and accepted.

You can't hide it. Your hsuband can sense it a mile away. I'm talking about that subtle thought you've probably had since you married: "I'll make him over someday." Sorry, but with that attitude, you probably won't.

Show him acceptance and understanding as he is. I'm not saying you have to accept his offensive ways without any hope of change. Just accept the fact that your husband needs to be taught—in creative ways—how to meet your needs.

FOR BETTER

Remember, you are *in the process* of teaching him, and he is *in the process* of learning. If you're on the same train, don't expect him to get there before you do.

Men need to know their advice is valuable.

If you can stay on the "right side" in the following ways, I believe you will demonstrate to your husband that his advice is valuable.

You shun his advice by . . .	You welcome his advice by . . .
picking up the newspaper or sewing while he's talking	putting aside all other interests while he's talking.
rolling your eyes.	giving him your full attention, eyes focused on him.
yawning.	pointing our positive or helpful aspects of his advice.
criticizing before you've heard him out.	letting him have the floor until he has fully expressed his opinion.
trying to get in the last word.	thanking him for the time he spent sharing his advice.

Men need to feel appreciated.

OR FOR BEST

Your husband probably feels that his biggest contribution to you and your family is the financial support he provides. Obviously, then, one of the best ways to show your appreciation for him is to thank him regularly for his diligence and faithfulness on the job. Even if you are providing part of the income, it is crucial that you show him how grateful you are for his provision.

Aside from financial support, your husband also demonstrates his care for you in "little ways." Maybe he keeps your car maintained, or perhaps he empties the trash twice a week. Try to keep a mental list of little things he does that save you time and effort. Then thank him for them as often as possible. When he feels he is meeting the "big and little" needs of his family, his self-respect increases. As a result, he will begin to feel a deeper love for his appreciative wife.

EXPLAIN YOUR UNIQUE NEEDS AND DESIRES

Make a list of the needs and desires you would like to see your husband fulfill. Divide your list into four categories: emotional needs, physical needs, spiritual needs, and mental needs. In some areas you may have an overflow of needs, and in others you may have to struggle to think of one need. But delve into your feelings until you believe your list is complete. Condense the list into the smallest number of vital needs so it doesn't appear overwhelming.

As you explain the list to your husband, remember to discuss one need at a time until you've covered each subject. Your husband may have trouble accepting the importance of some of your needs, so you may have to discuss the differences between men and women where sensitivity is concerned. But be sure to maintain the right attitude while explaining. When you appeal to him for understanding, avoid self-pity, jealousy, or whining. These approaches are repulsive to anyone, especially your husband.

Finally, as you begin to discuss your needs, be sure to use the salt principle when appropriate. Look for creative ways and times to share these needs. For example, you might want to write your husband a letter explaining a few of your deepest longings. Be careful not to accuse or imply failures on his part; just explain how you feel. Let him read it alone if he chooses. Be sure he can read it during a calm, tension-free time of the day.

The Worst Approach

One woman told me she was extremely discouraged about her husband's lack of interest in her. He had a tremendous drive and interest in his work, his friends, his pastimes, but almost no interest in her or their children. She talked on and on about how much she had tried to get him to change. Nothing seemed to work. When I discussed it with her husband, I found she had continually confronted him with his failures as a husband. He said she always seemed to choose the wrong time to talk about their problems—"Just when I was trying to unwind." To top it all off, she came across as a combination of prosecutor, judge, and jury. Just before he went to bed, just as he got home from work, almost anytime he "let down" around her, she started condemning and reasoning.

I began to see that she had what I call a "contentious spirit," *one that always contends for its own way.* She was constantly pushing him into a corner, trying to make him see her point of view. Even the Bible describes the effects of a contentious woman. She dries out a man like the searing desert sun; she drives a man to the corner of a rooftop; she drips on a man like a steady rain (Prov. 25:24; 21:19; 27:15).

What perfect analogies. Around the house, this woman's habits were as annoying as a constant dripping—like a leaky faucet. Her contention was like the sun beating down on a wayfarer in the desert. No matter where her husband turned, he couldn't get away from it. He found no oasis of relief because she continually reminded him of his failures. Finally, her actions had forced him to the corner of a rooftop with nowhere else to go.

Want to know what brought him down off the roof in a hurry? His wife got rid of her contentious spirit. Consequently, she inspired a tremendous change in her husband. Today she describes him as a much more loving husband who meets her needs in ways she never even dreamed possible.

Explaining your feelings and needs is not the same as voicing complaints. One couple, who constantly bickered, determined to go through a whole week without voicing any criticism. Rather than argue, each time either of them became irritated, they wrote it down. Each time either was annoyed by the other's failure, he or she wrote it down. They placed each "complaint" slip in one of two boxes, a "his" and a "her" box. At the end of the week, they planned to open the boxes. He would read her complaints and she would read his.

Saturday night finally arrived, and he decided to go first. He opened the box and began to read the dozens of little notes, one at a time. His eyes reflected the hurt and disappointment in himself as he read her complaints. "You've been promising to fix the screen door for six months, and it's still not fixed." "You never put your socks in the dirty clothes." "I'm getting sick and tired of having to pick up after you everywhere you go." He was sincerely grieved by all the ways he had offended his wife.

Then it was her turn. She opened the box and pulled out the first slip of paper. She read it with a lump in her throat. The next note brought tears to her eyes. Picking up three more notes, she read them quickly and began to weep. Every note in the box read, "I love you." "I love you." "I love you."

Like many wives, you may have been fooled into thinking that one day your complaints would finally remold your husband into the perfect mate. But I hope the example above clearly illustrates that unconditional love and tenderness, not complaints, can transform a cranky opponent into a humble, loving partner.

However, it is important to verbalize your feelings. One wife touched her husband's heart with a note she wrote him. He actually changed his weekly schedule to include more time with her. The note read: "Many days I feel like a shining little red apple—one of the top ones in a barrel. Everyday you come by and choose one, but never me. Your hand comes close, sometimes you even lift me up, but always you choose another. I've got a little worm growing inside me, and each day I become less attractive. I long for the day that you choose me!"

EXPRESS YOUR GRATEFULNESS WITHOUT EXPECTATIONS

Recently I received a card in the mail from my wife. In it, she said that she loved me, that every year of our marriage was more fulfilling, and that she appreciated some of my recent attitudes and actions. There were no hints of hidden expectations in the card. She didn't ask for a thing, but she sure made me want to do more for her.

Through the years, Norma's "no beg" attitude has inspired me to search for creative ways to express my love to her. And it all started with some tattered furniture in the early years of our marriage.

Norma was sick and tired of the pitiful "late garage" style furniture we owned. For months she begged me to replace it. "Gary, it's just awful. I'm so embarrassed when our friends come over. Ple-e-e-e-ase, can't we get some new furniture?"

I felt like a slave to her expectations. *No matter what I do, she'll never be satisfied,* I thought. *I'm not about to buy her any new furniture with that attitude.* (What a domineering attitude I had then!)

One day it dawned on me. *She hasn't said a word about that furniture for over a year. She hasn't even dropped hints about it.* Sure enough, Norma had completely given up her expectations to the Lord (Ps. 62:1–2). She started focusing more attention on her inner qualities. At that moment I was willing to do anything for her. I was so grateful for her "new" attitude that I asked her how much money *she* would like to withdraw from our savings account for new furniture. Then we marched down to the local furniture store and bought a couch, lamps, tables, chairs. . . .

Norma's complaints accomplished nothing, but her non-demanding patience accomplished everything. Around our house we've noticed several factors make it easier for any family member to change: expressing the change you desire to see without attaching a time limit; showing appreciation for the slightest move toward change; showing acceptance and love regardless of change.

FOR PERSONAL REFLECTION

Using 1 Peter 3:1–6,

1. Write out your own definitions of admiration, and
2. design one practical application for showing gratefulness this next week. See also 1 Thessalonians 5:18.

10

How To Gain Your Husband's Comfort And Understanding Instead Of Lectures And Criticism

"To sum up, let all be harmonious, sympathetic, brotherly, kindhearted, and humble in spirit; not returning evil for evil, or insult for insult, but giving a blessing."
1 Peter 3:8–9

It was the dead of winter, and Lois felt like she had been cooped up in the house for weeks. She had been invited to a women's luncheon so she jumped at the chance to get out of the house. She got in her car, turned the key, and to her dismay the battery was dead. Realizing her plans were ruined, she rummaged through her purse for the house keys. Suddenly she remembered she had left the keys inside the house. It was definitely "one of those days" . . . she couldn't go to the luncheon, she couldn't get into the house, her neighbors weren't home, and there wasn't a phone nearby. Her only choice was to trudge to a phone in the bitter weather. On the way, a high school student recognized her and offered her a ride. She decided to go to her husband's office instead. Discouraged and depressed, she needed her husband's comfort.

Enter husband—irritated and angry. He just couldn't believe she had locked herself out of the house. And to top it all off, she had the gall to embarrass him by coming to his office during work hours. Just so it wouldn't happen again, he let the harsh words fly. Of course, his words produced nothing but more frustration and hurt feelings in Lois.

Why do men find it so much easier to lecture their wives than to comfort them? If you could climb into a man's mind, you would see that when he is confused or hurt he seeks a *logical explanation* for his feelings. Once he has made a clear analysis of the problem, he usually feels relieved. It is only "logical," then, that he respond to your problems in the same way. In essence, he thinks he can "talk you out of it."

But if your relationship with your husband is to be strengthened, it's vitally important that he learn when and how to comfort you. You shouldn't feel guilty about your need for someone to "lean on." That need is not a sign of weakness, as some would have you believe. It's simply a part of our human nature. We all need to lean at times.

I believe there are least three steps you can take to increase his awareness of your need for tender comfort.

GET EXCITED OVER HIS ATTEMPTS TO COMFORT YOU

The first step in motivating your husband to comfort you is to respond in a big way each time he does the slightest thing to comfort you. This is called *positive reinforcement*. It demonstrates how much you appreciate his understanding. I'm not telling you to try out for cheerleader each time he comforts you. Just remember to do something special for him—maybe a day, even a week later. Perhaps a special meal, a romantic night in the bedroom, or an unexpected love note in his lunch box or wallet. If there was anything you particularly liked about the way he comforted you, call attention to it. Regardless of what you do to show your appreciation, be sure he sees the link between your gratefulness and his act of comfort. Incidentally, he needs to learn how to comfort you as much as you need to receive it. He needs it for his own personal well-being and joy (John 15:11; Col. 3:12–15).

It's extremely important that you never ridicule or belittle any of your husband's attempts to comfort you. Even when his attempts are inadequate, rather than calling attention to his failure, praise him for anything positive in his actions. (Even the attempt itself is a move in the right direction!) Never try to gain his comfort by criticizing him for not comforting you.

Imagine for a moment that your son has just been taken to the hospital. You need someone to lean on emotionally. The anxiety is almost more than you can bear, but your husband just stands there. You're thinking inside, *Why don't you just hold me and reassure me?* So you blurt it out, "Don't just stand there. Come here and hold me." Now you've called attention to his inadequacy, compounding the anxiety and concern he feels for your son. Unfortunately, his natural response is to resist all the more.

People always respond more favorably to positive reinforcement than to negatives such as criticism or ridicule. In building your relationship, it's of utmost importance that you praise him for his attempts to be a comfort to you. But that's just the first step in motivating him to offer his emotional support.

TEACH YOUR HUSBAND HOW TO COMFORT BY BEING HIS EXAMPLE

The second step goes back to a principle we discussed in the previous chapter—you reap what you sow. One of the most effective ways to teach your husband how to comfort you is to discover how he likes to be treated when he's down. Teach by example. When you sense that he is fearful or uncertain, ask him to tell you how he feels. Tell him you understand. If he reacts to you, saying something like, "Don't treat me like a little kid," then try another approach. Perhaps he feels unmanly or childish in your comforting arms. In that case, you can comfort him with your words and facial expressions. He won't resist when you learn to comfort him the way he needs to be comforted.

To some men, emotional support means taking their side in a conflict. For example, when John was in college, his fiancée broke their engagement and decided to marry one of his best friends. John's only consolation came when his roommate, Ted, responded with deep empathy: "John, I don't know what's wrong, but I know you're hurting. If you want to talk about it, or if there's anything I can do, just say so. If you don't want to talk about it and you want to be left alone, I'll just wait in the living room until you feel a little better."

John, touched by his roommate's concern, revealed that his ex-fiancée was marrying a friend. "I just need some time to be alone," he said.

When Ted walked into the other room, John overheard him say to his girl friend, "Your best friend Sue just went and got engaged to another guy. How do you like that?"

That was just the type of comfort John needed. His roommate really understood how he was feeling!

Try to detect the most meaningful ways to comfort your husband in each situation.

TELL HIM GENTLY HOW YOU DESIRE TO BE COMFORTED

The third step is to teach him how you, as a woman, need to be comforted. It's important to remember that his natural inclination may be to solve your problems "logically" so that they don't arise again. Much of this is covered in the book *If Only He Knew*, but chances are you'll still have to be his main teacher. After all, you're the one he is learning to comfort.

You may remember the story I told earlier about the wife who received a lecture virtually every time she needed comfort. She had to remind her husband four or five times, "Don't try to tell me why it happened. Just hold me." He finally got the message. Had she not persisted, he never would have learned how to comfort her. (One encouraging point: they had been married nine years before she tried to teach him how to comfort her, but it only took a few weeks for him to catch on.)

One woman who had left her husband said, "I just can't stand the thought of going back into that situation. He offends me in so many ways, and then he never comforts me when I need it. I just can't go back." I asked her if she would be willing to teach her husband how to comfort her. She gave me a funny look and asked, "What do you mean, teach him?"

"When you're in a stressful situation, or when you're discouraged, how do you want him to treat you?"

"I'd like him to put both arms around me and gently hold

me. Then I'd want him to tell me that he understood or at least that he was trying to understand."

"Well, why don't you teach him that?"

"You're kidding! He'd think I was crazy. And besides, why should I have to teach him? He should do it on his own. I'd feel stupid having to tell him things like that."

I changed my approach a little. "Has he ever said things to you like, 'Honey, I don't know what you want me to do when you're discouraged. Should I cry, or kiss you, or . . .?' "

Her eyes lit up and she said, "Yeah, it's amazing the number of times he's said that he didn't know what to do, or how to act, or what to say. I even remember him saying, 'You just tell me what you want me to do. But I always thought he was being sarcastic, and I was offended because he couldn't figure it out by himself. I thought if I had to tell him it really wouldn't mean anything anyway. Do you mean some men really need to be taught the little things, like how to hold a woman tenderly?"

My answer was an obvious "yes." A lot of men avoid soft words and tender comfort because they have never been taught how to use them. Also, they simply don't understand the positive effects they will have on their wives and the sense of well-being they themselves will receive. I have found that once a man has learned why and how to comfort, he gains a real appreciation for the role it plays in his marital relationship.

During most of our marriage, my wife could never expect to receive comfort from me whenever she made an embarrassing mistake. I usually ridiculed her or got upset. But eventually, she began to share with me her need for sympathy, compassion, and understanding. Just when I was starting to get the hang of it, my newly acquired knowledge was put to the royal test. I came home one Saturday to find my camper parked at an angle in the driveway—not unusual in itself. Unfortunately, a large section of the garage roof was lying next to it in the driveway. Like most men, the first thought that came to mind was money. How much would it cost to fix it all? I felt like going into the house and screaming at my wife for her carelessness.

As these thoughts raced through my mind, I recalled the many times she had told me how she needed to be treated in upsetting situations. I walked up to her, put my arm around her with a smile, and choked out the words, "I'll bet you really feel bad. Let's go into the house and talk about it. I don't want you to feel bad for my sake."

Inside, I held her for a minute without saying anything. She told me she had dreaded my reaction as much as the accident. "That's okay, honey," I said. "We'll fix it. Don't worry about it." The longer I held her and the more I comforted *her*, the better *we* felt.

When we walked out to survey the damage, I realized it wasn't as bad as it looked. The roof hadn't splintered; the part that fell had sheared off neatly like a puzzle piece. All that was needed were some nails and a little paint. Within a few minutes, a friend had heard about the accident and had driven into my driveway with a pickup and tools; in an hour we had it completely fixed.

When we were finished, I thought to myself, *A couple of hours ago I could have crushed my wife's spirit, strained our relationship, and made her feel like an idiot . . . all over an hour's work.*

Even though I thought Norma would be the only one to gain from my understanding attitude, in the long run I actually benefited the most. The increased admiration and respect I received from her provided an even greater incentive for comforting her. If you let your husband know that you deeply admire him for his comfort, he, too, will have an increased desire to comfort you.

FOR PERSONAL REFLECTION

Think of at least three future stressful situations that would cause you to desire comfort. Discuss these with your husband and explain exactly what you would need if any of the three situations occurred.

11

How To Motivate Your Husband To Receive Your Correction Without Defensiveness

"The heart of her husband trusts in her, and he will have no lack of gain."

Proverbs 31:11

"You pay more attention to that stupid dog than you do to me," Sheila yelled at her husband. "How can a grown man love a dog more than his wife?" Resentment had been gnawing at her for years since Bill took up the habit of playing with Peppy before bothering to say hello to her. Finally the anger and hurt burst through her self-control. Bill reacted with more anger. Another argument had begun.

In this chapter you will learn how Sheila could have handled her complaint to get the result she desired. Read and study the following seven ideas to learn how to motivate your husband to *accept correction* without a nasty argument or a defensive response. Then give them a try. We think you'll be in for a nice surprise.

FOR BETTER
USE THE "SANDWICH" APPROACH

Always layer your slice of correction between two pieces of praise. For example, if your husband complains that you overspend on the children's clothing, use the sandwich approach: First, the bread . . . "Honey, I really appreciate how hard you work to provide so many nice things for us. You really do love us." Next the meat (your correction) . . . "Sometimes I feel like you think I'm spending money frivolously, buying more clothes than the children need. I just want you to know that I really try to watch how much I spend, and I buy only what I think they need." And now the other slice of bread . . . "But most of all, I just want you to know how much we appreciate your hard work to make all this possible. The kids and I were talking about what a fantastic father and husband you are. . . ."

Usually, the apostle Paul began his letters with praise before he sandwiched in his reproofs. Look how he started the Book of Philippians: "I thank my God in all my remembrance of you" (1:3). Even defensive people are more receptive to correction when it's *cushioned with kind words*.

One policeman used to dread stopping speeders, even though it was part of his job, because of the hostility he encountered. He was miserable on the job until an older patrolman shared his secret. "Every time I pull someone over, I do something very important. It's the one thing that keeps me from getting negative reactions."

First, he approached the traffic violator with a smile. *Second*, he greeted him or her with a friendly "good morning" or "good afternoon." *Third*, he asked, "How's your day going?" with genuine concern. Usually the motorist would explain he had been having a miserable day. But by the time he told his problems to the interested patrolman, he was relaxed and congenial. Only then did the patrolman ask to see his license. After writing the ticket he would say, "I hope your day improves for you."

The younger policeman tried this approach and found it rarely failed. It can work for you and your husband too. Approach your husband with a smile and friendly words. Then find out what is troubling him. Once you've discovered the "burr under the saddle," you'll be much more understanding of his irritating behavior and better equipped to offer constructive criticism. Remember, a soft word turns away anger (Prov. 15:1). The more gentle and careful we are, the more others can receive our criticisms.

One caution about the sandwich approach. You should praise your husband from time to time without any corrective comments. Otherwise, he might become wary of "sandwiches."

TRY THE "PUZZLE" APPROACH

You can't put a jigsaw puzzle together without all the pieces, and you can't solve a problem without all the facts. (In Spanish the word for puzzle is *rompecabezas*, which literally means "break your head." And that's just what your husband feels like doing when you don't give him all the pieces.)

The more facts I have about a disagreement between Norma and me, the easier it is to find a clear solution to our problem. The first fact I obtain about her feelings or beliefs represents only one piece of the overall picture. When I lay it down on the table, it doesn't give me much of an idea about the finished picture. So, I add more pieces by asking questions, and the picture begins to take shape. Occasionally I try to force the wrong pieces together, but she lets me know when I do. Sometimes I try to guess what the completed picture will look like, but only when the pieces are fitted together do I know for sure. Often the finished picture (solution) is so simple that we wonder why we didn't see it right away.

Your husband can't put a solution together when you throw him one tidbit of information and stop at that. Nor can he wade through all the facts when you give him five hundred at once. Make it a point to give him one piece at a time until he has all the facts. (Simply give him the facts and let him draw his own conclusions.) When you don't focus on the consequences of his actions in a judgmental way, you'll be amazed how much easier he accepts correction. He may need a week, a month, six months, or more. The length of time depends on the individual problem, your attitude when you give him the pieces, and the strength of your relationship.

Incidentally, the puzzle approach is also useful when making personal decisions or helping your children learn to make sound decisions. Any fuzzy problem comes into focus when you take time to gather all the factors.

REPLACE "YOU" STATEMENTS WITH "I FEEL" STATEMENTS

Rather than expressing your feelings, "you" statements imply judgment and criticism; they place the blame on your husband. Try to replace "you" with "I feel."

Think back to the beginning of the chapter when Sheila accused Bill with, "You pay more attention to that stupid dog. . . ." Her "you" statement made her husband so angry and defensive they couldn't even discuss the problem. If she had used an "I feel" statement, the results would have been much different.

"Honey, I know that it's not intentional, but I feel like Peppy means more to you than I do. I know how ridiculous this must sound, but I just wanted you to know how I felt."

"Why do you feel that way?" he asked.

"Well, because when you come home from work, I feel you spend more time with Peppy than with me. This may sound insignificant, but if our relationship is going to grow and become all we want it to be, then it is important that I share my feelings."

Had the conversation continued, she could have gently shared a possible solution, but only at his request. "Why can't my husband come up with his own solutions?" you may ask. Unfortunately, some husbands probably wouldn't notice the problem if they tripped over it. In most cases, your husband will need a gentle nudge to notice and correct a problem.

MASTER THE "SALT PRINCIPLE"

Imagine that your husband is totally engrossed in a televised football game between two of the best teams in the nation. Then you make one statement that's enough to tear his attention away from the game and put it all on you. Impossible you say? Read on.

The "salt principle" stimulates your husband's interest in subjects he would otherwise find dull. The secret is in the manner of presentation. If you master the salt principle, he will practically beg to hear what you have to say, be it praise or correction. But you have to withhold your correction until you've created so much curiosity that he can't wait to hear it. The chart below illustrates the skillful use of the salt principle in correction.

Areas You Wish He Would Change	How to Tell Him By Asking Questions
He's too critical	"Honey, what bugs you the most about the bosses you've had?" If he mentions criticism, grouchiness, etc., ask him how it made him feel. He'll probably respond with, "It really took the life out of my job." Now the door is open for you to explain your feelings. "Honey, that's sort of how I feel when you're critical of me. It takes the life out of sex and makes it hard to respond to you physically."
He's too harsh.	"Honey, do you think it's possible for our relationship to improve every year?" "Yeah, sure I do." "Well, you know, if we could correct one *big* thing this year, I feel sure our relationship would be much more fulfilling. Would you be interested in hearing about it!" If he says yes, then you can respond with, "Honey, when you're harsh with me about something I've done wrong, I really feel like pulling back from you, especially when I'm already aware of my mistakes. I'd just love it if you would comfort me first, just hold me tenderly, and ask me how I'm feeling." If he says he is not in-

terested in hearing about that "one big thing," wait until later and add more salt to create greater curiosity and interest.

He ignores you.	"Honey, could we talk about how I can overcome some difficult feelings I have when we're at parties?" If he says yes, you might say, "Sometimes I feel all alone, just standing by myself while you're off with other people. I know you need those times with your friends, but I feel left out. What do you think we should do?" You might suggest a creative alternative. Perhaps at some social gatherings you could plan to stay with your husband while at others you could go off with friends. Or, you might decide on a balance of time together at each social event. Another solution might be to agree on a signal you could use at parties to show your husband you'd like to be with him more. The signal might be a move toward the group with whom he's talking or a casual glance at him across the room. As long as your husband agrees to this solution, you won't have to fear being called a "tag-along." And having talked it out before the party, you will feel more at ease, more secure, more involved while you're there.

SET AN EXAMPLE BY ENTHUSIASTICALLY RE-CEIVING HIS CORRECTION

An attitude of understanding and receiving his criticism not only is a wise decision, but will increase your love for him. That's what it says in Proverbs 9:8. When your husband finds fault with you, don't dig in your heels by offering a countercharge. Show him by example how to receive criticism without defensiveness. Admit that there is some degree of truth in his criticism, however small. When you're alone, reexamine his criticism and try to accept its valid points. Then get to work on the necessary changes. Talk about a heart melter! Nothing gets to the "perfect" husband faster than a pliable wife.

If you really want him to receive correction willingly, then actively *seek* constructive criticism from him. If you sense he is perturbed about something, ask him to tell you all about it. Draw him out about things you might have done to irritate him. When you see him building barriers between you, don't wait for him to explain. *Seek* his correction willingly. Only the wise seek reproof and they inherit honor (Prov. 3:35). We reap what we sow.

MAINTAIN OPEN COMMUNICATION WITH YOUR HUSBAND

Take down the barriers your offenses may have built by earnestly seeking your husband's forgiveness. Don't give him any excuse to avoid communication by leaving the lines crossed. It is crucial that you clear up each and every offense you cause if you want your husband to receive your correction in the future. Use your sensitivity to detect subsurface problems when your husband seems to shut you out, making sure there are no hidden barriers to your correction.

EXPLAIN WHY YOU NEED TO CORRECT HIM

I am often amazed at my wife's foresight, insight, perception, sensitivity . . . she foresees the consequences of my decisions long before I carry them out. Like most women, she perceives the subtle effects my decisions have on our home and children. I consider it her *responsibility* to share her observations with me. They are invaluable. By sharing your unique womanly insights, you afford your husband a special steering mechanism that can keep your whole family moving in the right direction. You may not have all the answers and you may not be right all the time, but your insight is a priceless resource to your husband. Explain to him in a tactful way that you would like to help him make the best decisions possible. Share with him that you sometimes notice different angles on a problem that he might be interested in. If you explain your insights in this way, he won't be threatened by a know-it-all attitude.

FOR PERSONAL REFLECTION

Read several chapters of Proverbs and notice the number of times Scripture encourages us to seek correction from others and why we should seek it. For example, try chapters 1, 12, and 13.

12

How To Gain Your Husband's Appreciation And Praise

"Her children rise up and bless her; her husband also, and he praises her."

Proverbs 31:28

"Hi, honey. Just a little note to tell you that I love you and miss you. Hurry back to me!"

John smiled to himself as he folded the note and put it back in his wallet. During his ten-year marriage he has had to travel a lot. He usually arrives at his hotel discouraged and lonely. But through the years his wife has made those times of separation a lot more pleasant by hiding cards, letters, even cookies in his suitcase.

"I get a warm feeling whenever I find a surprise," he says, "because I'm reminded of her love for me. It really makes me feel better, though I still miss her."

John kept one of her notes in his billfold during his last business trip. Whenever he was down, he took it out and reread it. The note was a constant reminder of her love and appreciation for him.

John's wife gained his praise and appreciation by freely showing appreciation for him. I have found that everyone has a deep hunger for praise and appreciation. Never in all my years of counseling have I heard a woman complain of too much praise from her husband.

But I have heard the opposite. "My husband is always so critical. If he would only appreciate the things I do." Though many wives may feel there is no hope, I know a husband can learn to praise his wife. I have found two ways a woman can increase her husband's appreciation for her and at the same time stimulate his outward expression of appreciation.

SHOWING APPROVAL FOR YOUR HUSBAND

As you read earlier, men hunger for appreciation from others. They will gladly receive recognition from secretaries, employers, employees, friends, or anyone else willing to give it. A man's need for approval is as strong as your need for security in financial matters and family relationships. When a man knows his wife approves of him, he enjoys her companionship. He will find himself spontaneously complimenting her in response to the approval she gives.

Instead of demanding appreciation from your husband or shedding tears when he doesn't give it, try the approaches suggested below.

The Direct Approach

One way to show approval is the "direct" approach—expressing esteem for your husband verbally or through letters, love notes, and cards. I'm looking at two cards my wife sent me last month. In the past, I would have opened them and thought, "Isn't that nice?" before tossing them into the nearest trash can. But the more cards and letters I receive from Norma, the more anxious I am to reciprocate her "written praise." Now when I receive a note from her, I usually keep it for several readings. When she sends cards that cite specific qualities she appreciates in me, I feel inspired to think about her praiseworthy qualities and reciprocate with a card.

Though it's true that all men need appreciation, not all men like the same *form* of appreciation. Be careful to avoid forms your husband might find gushy or overly sentimental. You can discern what will encourage your husband and what will embarrass him by trying several ways until a few really hit home.

My heart goes out to one Baylor University coed who hired a fraternity group to sing a Valentine love song to her fiancé. She expected him to react dramatically to the surprise she planned, but he never mentioned it to her.

"Jim, how did you like your Valentine song?" she finally asked.

"Oh, yeah," he said. "I heard it, but I didn't really understand why you did it. It was kind of confusing to me."

His response left her hurt and confused. She honestly wondered if he cared for her at all. This pointed example illustrates something I hope each woman will remember long after this book has been read: men think differently than women.

The exercise below will help you learn how to show approval for your husband. In the left column, list ten admirable areas of his life. In the right column, record how you intend to praise him in that area. You may want to tell him personally or with a special note hidden where he'll be sure to find it. However you choose to do it, let it be your way of saying, "Honey, I really approve of what you've done and who you are." Remember, we can value someone even if they irritate us.

FOR BETTER

Things You Approve of About Your Husband	Direct and Creative Ways to Show Your Approval
1. _____	_____
2. _____	_____
3. _____	_____
4. _____	_____
5. _____	_____
6. _____	_____
7. _____	_____
8. _____	_____
9. _____	_____
10. _____	_____

The Indirect Approach

The "indirect" approach is another way to show approval for your husband. Husbands and wives were using this approach long before the flood of marriage books hit the market.

Norma's mother had this approach down pat years ago. Through good grooming and an encouraging 5:00 P.M. greeting, she showed "indirect" approval for her husband. Every day she prepared for his homecoming by bathing and putting on fresh clothing. Norma says she can't remember a single time when her mother greeted her father with problems or complaints. Instead, she let him relax and made him feel important by the extra time and effort she spent to make one part of his day happy.

Norma's mom was a good teacher. I have never come home to the wife portrayed in cartoons—dressed in a sagging, torn housecoat and curlers as permanent as light fixtures. Norma always looks good and smells good.

I could list thousands of indirect ways to show approval for your husband. Norma knows plenty of them. Just to name a few: she welcomes my suggestions about her wardrobe; she introduces me to new friends with a tone of voice that reflects admiration for me; and she constantly tells our children how much she appreciates me.

I remember the time when I came home from work dead on my feet, too tired to protest when my daughter climbed into my lap with sticky fingers. "Daddy, mommy says you work real hard to take good care of us." A warm sensation spread over me, and suddenly I didn't feel so tired. (Chances are, your children will let your husband know what's being said "behind his back." I hope for his sake that it's good.)

Praise your husband to his male friends and their wives. Just think what good gossip you'll spread when you say positive things about your spouse. Quite a switch from the usual complaints!

At this point, make a long list of the indirect ways you can show approval for your husband. Pick two or three of the best ones and be sure to apply them during the next week.

Three Ways to Alienate Your Husband

Wives often alienate their husbands by *unknowingly expressing disapproval of them.* Here's how one woman's disapproval drove a wedge between herself and her husband.

Joan always greeted Frank at the door with pushy advice about this problem or that decision. He began to dread his homecoming each day because he envisioned Joan as a stalking lion, ready to pounce on him.

One evening, before he could even put down his briefcase, Joan pounced. "I heard what you said to the Jacksons at the company party. I thought about it all day." Frank's stomach knotted in a hot wad as he blocked out her words. But her shrill voice pierced his defense. "Frank! Frank! You never listen to me. I want you to call the Jacksons right now and invite them to dinner next week. We have to be friends with them if you ever want to get anywhere in the company."

I can't believe she thinks I'm so dumb, Frank thought. *Why does she keep pushing me?*

A man often interprets his wife's bossiness as a lack of approval. *She must not think I'm too capable, judging from all the advice she gives me.*

In defense of many wives, I recognize that the passive nature of the typical husband forces a wife to "take over." I hear how very frustrating it is for you. My encouragement is that a natural response doesn't always gain the result you desire. Another paraphrase of Ephesians 5:22 is, "Let your husband take care of your needs just as you allow the Lord to love you."

Another way wives show disapproval for their husbands is by *discrediting their feelings or desires.* As a highly skilled art critic, one wife decides to quietly dispose of his pitiful Rembrandt reproduction. As an expert seamstress, another wife criticizes that "custom-made" suit he got on sale. Or, on a more realistic plane, the veteran gardener ignores her husband's desire to plant a pine tree on the front lawn and opts for a maple instead.

If you will listen closely, you can hear your husband expressing his desires every hour. Right now he may be mumbling behind his newspaper about chicken spaghetti with sour sauce and cherries on top like his mother used to make. Pick up on his subtle statement and make it for him. If you don't, he'll wonder whether he's worth anything to you. Resentment may spring up alongside his doubt, and soon he'll make unconscious efforts to eliminate things that please you. "I know what you want, but I don't want to do it" becomes the sad response of many husbands.

You may have to run on sheer willpower to respond to your husband's desires at first. But remember, good feelings usually follow loving actions. Who knows? You may even learn to like his mother's chicken spaghetti concoction.

As proof of your good intentions, write down at least ten things you know are important to your husband. Schedule one or two a week for him. The best way to obtain a completely accurate list is to ask him. "Honey, I'd like to sit down and find out what things in life are really important to you." His response may provide a list that will outlast your retirement years.

The third and most common way wives show disapproval of their husbands is by *contradicting them.* Have you ever sympathized with a husband who could hardly get a word out of his mouth before his wife jumped in with both feet to correct him. "No, that's not the way it was. It was like this. . . ."

Contradiction is hardly an invitation to most husbands. No one wants to live with a know-it-all.

When Frank and Mary came to my office for marital counseling, she was by far the more "motivated" of the two. She not only answered the questions addressed to her but also those addressed to her husband.

"Now, Frank," I asked, "how do you see the situation?"

Before Frank could utter a sound, Mary would interrupt and say, "He'll say something about me, but it won't be true. He exaggerates."

I rarely become irritated in counseling sessions, but this time I began to boil within.

I asked, "Frank, what do you think the problem is?" and Mary said, "I think it's that he never spends any time with me."

Time after time, Mary answered Frank's questions. Even when he did speak up for himself, Mary had a countercharge that put him to shame. Several perplexing questions came to mind. Was the woman deaf? Had I misunderstood them when they introduced themselves—was her name Frank and his Mary?

This kind of problem usually indicates a very passive, non-communicative husband. She's had to answer for him if any type of communication was to occur between them. However, after a while he interprets this method as a put-down.

I suggest that with this type of person you: 1) direct questions to him in a loving, accepting manner to draw him out; 2) wait for him to express himself; 3) praise him for each genuine idea he expresses.

List the ways you have contradicted your husband lately and make a silent promise to forsake them in the future. Each time you are tempted to contradict him in front of someone, step into his shoes and imagine the embarrassment he will feel.

GENTLY TEACH YOUR HUSBAND ABOUT YOUR NEED FOR HIS APPROVAL

Judy loved teaching because her principal commended her regularly for her skills and methods. Rarely did a day pass without a gentle, encouraging word from him. It seemed the more he praised her work, the better she became.

Imagine the effect constant praise would have on your attitude as a wife. You would work harder each day to BE the mate your husband talked about. You would also be absolutely free to praise him once you knew your work was appreciated. Don't be embarrassed to request his praise. There's nothing wrong with the boost you receive from sincere praise.

Norma once overheard a grocery store clerk explain how much she loved her job because the friendliness of the customers made her feel accepted and needed. "And my boss and the other clerks tell me I do a good job, too," she said. "I'd rather be here where somebody appreciates me than at home with that husband of mine. Even if I fix a ten-course meal, he doesn't notice. But just let me be late with dinner once! Then I hear about it."

This woman needed to admit her need for his approval. If a woman can't admit her need for praise, then her marriage will become stale and superficial. Her feelings of love and responsiveness will dry up, and she will start building walls to keep her husband at a distance. A woman will never completely feel like her husband's helper and completer until she *hears* how she is helping and completing (Gen. 2:18).

Be specific with your husband about *when* you need his praise. Try something like, "I know you want a happy marriage. Dear, would you like to know what you can do to make me a very happy wife? It won't cost you a thing. No energy— just a little creativity."

"What?"

"You can show your approval of me by praising me for who I am and what I do. For instance, I especially need your praise when I fix a special meal for you or go out of my way to do something extra. I just need to know how you liked it. I need it, and it's okay to need it."

Perhaps you can best explain your need for appreciation

by relating it to one of your husband's personal experiences. When one husband asked his wife why she wouldn't take a vacation with him, she responded, "Would you want to take a vacation with your old boss?" (He had just quit his job due to harsh criticism from his boss.)

His wife gently explained, "When you criticize me, I feel like you do when your boss criticizes you. I feel defeated when you ignore the good things about my meals and point out what I forgot, like—"The salt isn't on the table," or "You didn't buy the right kind of butter. Even though we both have jobs, I feel you expect me to fix dinner while you watch television. I feel less than a person."

Dale broke down and cried. Within six months, he was a completely different person. Having conquered the temptation to complain, he is now free to meet his wife's need for approval and praise.

LIGHT UP WHEN HE PRAISES YOU

The last way to teach your husband about your need for approval is to "light up" whenever he praises you. Reward him with enthusiasm and excitement, making him subconsciously desirous of praising you more often.

As human beings, we all need and respond to praise. There is nothing shameful about longing for an occasional "pat on the back." So, demonstrate your legitimate need by responding to your husband's praise with a cheerful face and bright expressions. He will be sure to remember it next time you need approval.

OR FOR BEST
FOR PERSONAL REFLECTION

Memorize Ephesians 4:29. List the words you can use to build up (edify) your husband. Then list the words that tear him down so you can avoid these. What comes out of our mouths should encourage and lift another (Ephesians 4:29).

13

How To Help Your Husband Share Responsibility For Your Children And The Household Needs

"The ones who are married, they are concerned about how they may please one another" (paraphrased).
1 Corinthians 7:33–34

When your husband bolts through the door at 5:00 P.M., where is he headed? What does he look forward to after work each day? A snooze underneath the newspaper in his easy chair? Maybe a good hour with the sawdust and skill saws in his workshop?

Is it so unrealistic to wish that he looked forward to being with *you* in the evenings, helping with the children and household responsibilities? No, it's not. I believe this chapter will help you to motivate your husband to strengthen his relationship with you by *sharing* responsibilities for the house and children. In other words, it will help your husband think in terms of doing things *with* you rather than leaving the whole "job" to you.

Dr. James Dobson, a leading psychologist, says his real work in life begins when he gets home at night—helping his wife with the children and developing relationships with them through meaningful activities. I would like all men everywhere, including your husband, to be a part of one of life's greatest challenges and obligations—family life. Here are four ways to increase his desire to "join the family."

CREATIVELY EXPLAIN YOUR NEED FOR HIS HELP

In general, a man doesn't understand a woman's need for help with the children and household responsibilities. Also, he may not understand how his neglectful ways affect your feelings of "going it alone."

The only way your husband *may* ever understand you is for you to explain it to him. Many women, fearing ridicule, are ashamed to tell their husbands when they are physically exhausted. Once while lecturing on this subject I described the tremendous fatigue many women endure raising preschool children. A woman in the audience later told me that as I spoke she literally relived the pain of raising three children without her husband's help. Not only had she suffered physical exhaustion, but emotional anguish as well when her husband belittled her duties in comparison to his in the "hard business world."

Due to the widespread misinformation about homemaking, many women shudder to admit their occupations as housewives. They feel like martyrs or second-class citizens. If a husband detects these attitudes in his wife, he too will begin to look on her with disdain. Soon his sarcastic verbal and nonverbal communication will cut into her inner-being, damaging her self-image severely.

You must paint a picture of yourself for your husband's benefit. Let it portray your physical limitations and your unique needs. Without it your husband may expect more than you're able to give. Paint another picture for him that shows exactly what you do around the house and with the children. Explain how many times a day you change your son's diapers, chase the children out of the street, and pick up after them. Help him picture the fatigue and pressure you face, knowing you'll never catch up with the housework. Open his eyes to the boredom you feel as you fold and refold, straighten and restraighten, tie and retie. Then tell him about the mental drain of answering hundreds of, "Mommy, can I . . .?" questions.

While my coauthor put into words the daily tasks many women face, he said he felt an overwhelming grief about how blind he has been to his wife's hard work the last nine years. "Gary, I can't let her do all of this by herself," he said. "She's told me about these things for years, but I never realized till now what she's really been going through. As I think back, I've heard or seen her do every single thing you mentioned."

I learned the greatest lesson of my life not in college or graduate school but right in my own home. In one single lesson, I gained a deep understanding of what my wife goes through every day of her life. If every husband in America could undergo my experience, the wives in America would be enthroned as queens. What was the lesson? My wife had major surgery and spent two weeks in the hospital. During that time I took care of all three of our children. I cooked the meals—all forty-two of them, not counting the eighty-four snacks in between. And I attempted to fulfill the thousands of household responsibilities in my "spare time." I soon realized it would take all I had just to keep up with the kids and do "surface" cleaning. I couldn't do half the work my wife normally did. One day she asked, "Have you been able to clean out the closet?" Clean the closet? Good grief, I had been stuffing things in the closet just to get them out of the way! Once I even lost one of the kids and found him lodged between the basketball and the dirty clothes! "Honey, I haven't had time to clean out the closet. I'm exhausted!" I responded. All those additional tasks she crammed into her schedule made me realize how frustrating and exhausting housework can be without help.

I'm sure you realize that the average husband gets up Sunday morning, dresses himself, expects breakfast and glares because his wife isn't ready on time for church—while she's supervised dressing the children and everything else that goes into the preparation. Many of us men haven't even noticed it.

Perhaps you are one of the few completely organized women who can keep her household in perfect order with no assistance. I don't see how any woman can do that unless she neglects everything else in life to become the family maid. It would be far less backbreaking to gain your family's support in housekeeping. Try the following simple suggestion: Make it a game for each family member to pick up one misplaced item each time he or she leaves a room. That way, no one has to pick up everything, but everyone picks up something. And you don't have to face the frustration of straightening the house each time your family "blows through."

Another suggestion: Once you've explained your need for his help, appeal to your husband for help on the basis of his physical *strength* and *stamina*. Let him know when you need his strength to move a dresser or lift a heavy box. Tell him how much more lively you would be in the evening if he joined with you in your many projects. And remember, share your needs in a gentle, non-threatening way.

One newlywed husband snubbed his wife's request to help with the dishes. Frankly, he considered it beneath him. His mother had never expected that kind of help from his father.

Besides, the dishes were her job. He worked all day and figured he had a right to come home and relax. He had his job and she had hers. *She probably sees an easy way out of her job now that I'm around,* he thought. But his attitude changed immediately when his wife finally explained that she just wanted to be with him, to talk to him and enjoy his company.

It's likely your father-in-law didn't help his wife around the house. If that's the case, your husband probably feels housework is unmanly. He may fear getting caught in the disgraceful act by friends or relatives and being tagged "henpecked" for the rest of his life. Or, he may simply doubt your need for help as he remembers his mother's "Lone Ranger" abilities.

Let me give you an example of how to empathize with your husband in this area: "Honey, I want you to know how much I appreciate your hard work. I realize you probably don't feel like helping me around the house after a hard day's work, but it sure would help me to meet your needs as a wife if you could do some things *with* me. Besides your physical help around the house, I'd also enjoy your company. You're just fun to be with."

After such a gentle suggestion, if your husband implies you've concocted a clever plan to get him to do your work, then try again another time. This is the perfect opportunity to express two of the inner qualities we talked about earlier—courage and persistance. Keep explaining in a gentle, creative way how much you need his at-home involvement, especially if you're working outside the home.

Looking back, I now see the damage I caused in my own marriage by expecting my wife to do what she was never made to do. I "forced" her to labor beyond her physical capacity, expecting her to help me maintain the yard, carry furniture, lift heavy boxes; I often even added errands to her overloaded schedule, thinking she had plenty of free time. And to make sure she wasn't loafing, I played Inspector General. "Norma, tell me what you got done today." If I had only known then what I know now!

A close friend shared my sentiments recently as he recalled the birth of his second child. Calloused and ignorant of women's needs, he let his wife resume her normal chores too soon after a very difficult childbirth. For the next three years she endured severe pain until she finally had to have major surgery. He said he now realizes that the pain and mental anguish she suffered could have been easily prevented by his tender understanding and help.

Remember, you're doing him a big favor by helping him *understand* you. "Husbands . . . live with your wives in an understanding way . . . and grant her honor . . . so that your prayers may not be hindered (1 Peter 3:7).

EXPLAIN HOW HIS HELP WILL BRING LASTING BENEFITS TO YOUR CHILDREN

Many child psychiatrists say children desperately need to see a genuine loving relationship between their parents. They have found that children who see a deep affection between their parents have fewer mental and emotional problems in life. Children whose parents are in conflict can lose their self-worth and can slip downhill into psychological problems.

The answer is not to focus all your affection on your children. Dr. Alfred A. Nesser of Emory University School of Medicine warns against centering the family primarily around love for the children. He believes even a longstanding marriage can disintegrate if the husband or wife gives more love to the children than to his or her mate. In the book

Seven Things Children Need, John M. Drescher said, "The wife who loves her children more than her husband is endangering *both* her children and her marriage."

For your children's sake, it is crucial that you and your husband do everything possible to strengthen your love relationship. One of the best ways to demonstrate your love for each other is to do things together around the house. While you enjoy your husband's company, your children will be developing self-worth and security in the knowledge of their parents' healthy relationship.

MOTIVATING HIM TO HELP BY SHOWING ENTHUSIASM FOR HIS HELP

Throughout this book we've stressed the importance of expressing approval through praise or other indirect methods. Perhaps the most forceful method is "lighting up"— showing enthusiastic appreciation with an appropriate facial expression. When you "light up" in response to your husband's help, you not only increase his feelings of self-worth, but you provide an incentive for him to help you in the future.

I've heard many wives say, "Whenever my husband helps around the house, he makes such a big deal out of it that I'd just as soon do it myself." Those women are forgetting that it *is* a big deal to him. He really believes any work he does after 5:00 is "overtime." Whenever he does a chore at home, large or small, he probably feels he's the greatest husband in the world. Don't pop his balloon by belittling his help. Instead, praise him and show genuine appreciation. Tell him you think he's extra-special since many husbands won't help their wives at all. Your praise will deepen his love for you and increase his desire to help you.

My mother had a knack for making me feel special. A widow for many years, she often needed my help around the house so she could work to support our family. Whenever I came home from school, the kitchen cupboard was usually stacked with breakfast and lunch dishes. Occasionally I cleaned up the mess, doing the best "little boy" job I could. When my mother came home from work and found it clean, she lit up with vivacious facial expressions. Then she felt my forehead, acting as though she thought I was sick. She never criticized my job, though I spilled plenty of water and broke a few dishes. She made such a big deal out of my little chore that I really felt great. The appreciation she showed made it all worthwhile.

When your husband does a "big thing" around the house, you can take one of two approaches. You can either drive him out with what he did wrong or draw him in with what he did right. Don't give your husband any excuse to avoid helping you in the future—no wrinkled brow, no disgusted grunt. Those of you who lean toward perfectionism will have to go extra-heavy on the patience until your husband learns how you want it done. Just accept his help, whatever its form, and correct it later.

And remember: It's never too late to change. One husband refused to help his wife with any household duties during nineteen years of marriage. But a personal crisis motivated him to change within three months. Now he clears the table after each meal and looks forward to washing the dishes with his wife. He also helps her with the laundry from start to finish. (His wife could have lost ground in their relationship by insisting on her special towel-folding method. Instead, she had fun showing him how to do it until he finally learned her way.)

GAINING HIS HELP BY INTRODUCING HIM TO A REAL "MAN'S MAN"

One summer several years ago our family took a short vacation at a lakeside resort. We felt we needed a rest from all the pressures at home, a nice "family only" time together. But it didn't turn out to be just family. At the resort I met another husband whose relationship with his wife made such an impression on me that from then on I enjoyed helping my wife at home and with the children.

Strong and athletic, this man was a professional coach whom I had admired at a distance for some time. I enjoyed everything about him except the way he treated his wife. You'd think she was a queen the way he helped her. For one shocking week I watched him help prepare meals, set the table, and clean the table. He frequently offered to help without being asked and always took the major role in correcting the children rather than expecting her to assume total responsibility. Once he even encouraged his wife to read a book while he did the chores. Did he ever show me up! Next to him, I felt like such a failure as a husband and father that I almost wished I could pack up and go home.

You might suspect that his wife acted like she ran the show. Not so. She obviously loved him deeply and showed sincere respect for him at all times. She treated her husband as I wanted my wife to treat me. But I didn't dare compare her to Norma. After all, how could I expect that kind of treatment when I wasn't willing to give the same?

Maybe this "man's man" wasn't so dumb to put on an

apron and bury his arms in dishwater. As I watched him with his wife and saw the love they shared, I began to realize I was the real dummy. If I wanted my wife to treat me like his wife treated him, then I would have to earn it. Many times I have been grateful for that man's tremendous example.

You may not know anyone like him, but keep your eyes open for a man whom your husband respects. If that man treats his wife the way you want to be treated, then try to spend more time with the couple so your husband can benefit from his example. However, *never* push your husband to change by comparing him to the other man. Believe me, your husband is much more likely to change as *he notices* his friend's living example.

GAINING HIS HELP WITH A SUGGESTED "HONEY-DO" LIST

Some husbands won't like my next suggestion at all. However, many will find it helpful in learning how to get involved in their wives' household responsibilities.

My wife frequently gives me a list of four or five jobs she needs help with on Saturdays or after work hours. She's always careful not to overwhelm me with too many tasks per list. And she always explains any details about the list that would otherwise be unclear. Like, "Honey, the doorknob I wanted you to install wasn't available at the hardware store so I need you to order it from the catalog." I happen to enjoy fixing mechanical things, but your husband might not. If that is the case, don't put jobs on his list that are frustrating and/or impossible for him. Give him enough jobs to get him involved and lighten your load but not so many that he dreads your next list. And above all, try to include jobs he can do *with* you.

Once you've made your list, stimulate your husband's curiosity about it. Explain how his help will directly improve your relationship, make it easier to meet his needs, etc. If he still reacts negatively, either drop the idea for a while or decrease the number of tasks until he begins to see the benefits of helping you.

FOR PERSONAL REFLECTION

As you pray that your husband will fully understand you and your motives to *share* your life with him, including the household responsibilities, learn the deep meaning found in Luke 18:1–6. With a calm spirit of expectancy from the Lord, patiently approach the Lord with your requests. And with this same spirit, approach your husband.

14

How To Motivate Your Husband
To Meet Your Material Needs

"Be anxious for nothing, but in everything by prayer and supplication with thanksgiving let your requests be made known to God."

Philippians 4:6

Perhaps the first thing newlyweds learn is that two can live as cheaply as one—for half as long. Getting lifestyle in line with income is a tough requirement during those first years of marriage. It often sparks a war that can end in divorce court.

What one partner finds an absolute necessity, the other views as an unnecessary luxury. She may have kept a weekly hairdo appointment since the time she could walk. And her fashion-conscious husband may have been adding a shirt and tie to his wardrobe each month for the past fifteen years. So we're off to war over twenty-five dollars left in the till at the end of the month. He just has to have a new shirt and tie, and she knows she'll become the laughingstock of the community if she doesn't get her hair done. Husbands whose wives don't work outside the home often feel it's "my money" and rationalize with statements like, "If I'm going to be respected on my job, I have to look and feel successful." State-

173

ments like that can send a wife down Guilt Boulevard. She begins to feel guilty about wanting anything for herself. That, of course, is a primary motivation for women to seek outside employment—"So I can earn my own money." But even those wives who stick to the necessities may feel they have to justify or explain where each penny went. Their husbands may gladly fork over four or five hundred for a new toy and then grill their wives over a ten-dollar extra on the grocery bill.

Since their environment becomes an integral part of their lives, women often suffer depression when their homes are not an expression of themselves but an expression of what they can afford. "That picture is not my taste. It's just my budget." Obviously the solution is not an extravagant shopping spree to make your home the perfect illustration of you. However, you can gain the freedom to make your home an expression of yourself one step at a time. I am not suggesting that you neglect your family's basic needs in favor of home improvement. But it is possible that a portion of your husband's paycheck can be channeled toward your needs. This chapter will give you the essential tools to motivate your husband to cheerfully meet your needs as a wife, a mother, an individual, and a homemaker. After all, providing for his family is a basic biblical responsibility (1 Tim. 5:8).

Through the years I have pinpointed five ways husbands have been successfully motivated to meet their wives' needs. These five will not necessarily have the same effect on all men, so you will need to determine which approach has the best potential for your husband. For many of you, trial and error may be the only way to discover the best approach.

EXPRESS YOUR MATERIAL NEEDS WITH CONVICTION AND ENTHUSIASM

For twenty years, Carol had "beat around the bush" when expressing material needs to her husband, Ken. Like many women, she feared the "third degree." Her husband had established a dependable routine of questions for those times when she expressed needs. As a result, Carol had developed a dependable justification which she used to prepare Ken for every need. Hardly a positive approach, hers was like a whimpering puppy's. She was always painfully mindful of her last "offensive" request and even more afraid of making another. Her husband usually responded with little or no interest. When he did give in and give her some money, his begrudging attitude made her feel even worse. But she finally grew tired of her approach and his response, realizing she was a worthwhile individual with opinions and ideas as valid as his. So, she decided to begin expressing her needs in a direct, positive way. Without apology or explanation, she said with a smile, "Dear, I need to buy a new coat for Tommy. It's getting cold, and the other one is worn out. I need thirty dollars because I'm going to buy it today."

She was shocked by her husband's response. "Hey, that's great. Thanks for taking care of it." He gave her the money, no questions asked. (Keep in mind that money was no problem for Ken. He had plenty of it, but kept it in a tight fist.) All it took was a logical presentation with confidence and conviction on Carol's part. Once Ken sensed the urgency of the need, he was willing to loosen up and meet it.

Many women meet less resistance, criticism, and questioning when they express their needs directly to their husbands. Though the direct approach may fail with some husbands,

I do know it works on me. I really appreciate my wife's straightforward, enthusiastic, and logical way of expressing the needs of our family. "Conviction and influence" is the Hebrew meaning of the "virtuous" woman described in Proverbs 31:10–31.

Even outside my home I am influenced daily by this principle. When people approach me with a long preamble of excuses, invariably I lose interest in helping them. Their excuses attach a "low priority" tag to their needs as far as my time is concerned. When I hear, "Mr. Smalley, I really would like to talk to you but I hate to take up your time," I think to myself, *I'm really too busy to help him.* On the other hand, when people ask for my time with conviction and enthusiasm, I am usually eager to meet with them. "Gary, I've come up against a tough problem, and I need some answers right away. I wanted to get moving on it, and I know you're the person to help me. Could you take some time? It's very important." Of course I will. I get enthused about helping people like that because I know they are ready for a solution. They are coming to talk because they want answers right away.

Here again we can focus on the value of women. Since women appear to be more observant about relationships, it would be reasonable to assume that you more readily notice the special physical needs of your family and your children. And since men tend to be more preoccupied with their vocation, they need reminders. Recognize your strength and let your husband *see* your convictions and enthusiasm.

Let me also remind you that timing and attitude are crucial to the effectiveness of this approach. Be particularly sensitive to your husband's state of mind before you approach the subject of needs. He may need time to relax, take a shower, or jog before you begin the discussion. Once he's ready, share your needs and your feelings honestly but not critically. Take care not to accuse your husband of being unconcerned. Above all, avoid anger. It can provoke your husband to dig in his heels and rationalize his attitudes more than ever.

An enthusiastic attitude can evoke just the opposite response. When a husband picks up his wife's contagious enthusiasm, he too will consider her needs top priority. Get the enthusiasm flowing by recognizing that your needs are valid and worth expressing with confidence. Your husband will notice the difference and begin to acknowledge your special awareness of needs.

APPEAL TO HIS SENSE OF LOGIC

Most men require an orderly presentation of facts before they can make a decision. That's why it's important that you learn how to express needs in a way he can "process" them. Any time you want to present a need to your husband, ask yourself the following four questions:

1. Why do I need it?
2. What is the best product on the market?
3. Where can I buy it for the lowest price?
4. What will be the consequences if I don't buy it now?

Why do I need it?

This question will help your husband see the benefits of the purchase you want to make. Even a new dress or a beauty shop appointment for you can have positive effects on your husband and family. What may appear a selfish request on

177

your part is often a potential benefit for your family. How so? Don't you feel 100 percent better with a new hairdo? Doesn't it affect the way you treat your children and your husband at the dinner table? If so, all you have to do is record *why* you want to make a particular purchase and the positive effects it will have on your husband and family. Then simply present the facts in a calm, orderly manner.

What is the best product on the market?

Even though you've finally decided you really need that sofa, you're not quite ready to approach your husband. Now you must discover the most effective way to meet the need over the long run at the lowest cost. You should decide on the style and brand that will give you the longest life at the lowest expenditure. The cheapest sometimes ends up being the most expensive. For example, one sofa may seem a bargain at $400. But if it is constructed so cheaply that it lasts for only two years, the pro-rated cost of that "bargain sofa" is $200 a year. On the other hand, a higher quality sofa may cost you $600 and last six years. Although it cost $200 more initially, in the long run it costs only $100 a year. I'm not suggesting that the highest quality merchandise is always best for you. Many of your purchases will be limited by your income. However, if you can postpone your purchase and save for the best long-term buy, you will demonstrate wisdom and business ability to your husband. And the fact that you've researched the available products will impress him with the seriousness of the need. Telephone several stores and ask a salesperson to give you the brand names of the best merchandise. After several calls, one brand may be mentioned as the best by four or five salespeople.

* * *

OR FOR BEST

Where can I buy it for the lowest price?

I doubt that you need help in this area. Most women are excellent shoppers. The one thing I do want to point out, though, is that your husband needs to know you have checked the prices in *several* stores. I'm always impressed when Norma can show me the high price tags in three or four stores and then the low price tag where she intends to make a purchase. It makes me feel more secure, knowing she's not getting taken by a salesperson. Comparative shopping, since it takes time and effort, proves that my wife isn't on an impulse-buying spree.

What will be the consequences if I don't buy it now?

As you consider the answers to this question, the weak supports for your need will fall away, hopefully leaving the genuine urgency for it. Thoughtful consideration may reveal you really don't need to make the purchase in the time frame you originally established. If that is the case, the time pressure will be lifted like a burden from your shoulders. On the other hand, you may discover serious consequences that would result by not making the purchase immediately. That kind of evidence would communicate the urgency of the need to any husband.

After you have the answers to each of these four questions, you should be ready to make a logical presentation to your husband. If after plenty of research you still don't know which item to buy or where to buy it, then get your husband in on the act. Anything you can do together will strengthen your relationship.

EXPRESS GRATEFULNESS FOR THE NEEDS HE HAS ALREADY MET

There are plenty of creative ways to express gratefulness for the material needs your husband has met. One wife expressed gratefulness by getting rid of a piece of furniture her husband hated. When he noticed it was gone, she told him she had disposed of it to express appreciation for the way he had met a family need.

LEARN TO BE SATISFIED WITH YOUR HUSBAND ALONE

For years I was burdened with my wife's material expectations and had little motivation to meet her needs the way she desired. But suddenly she changed course. Nearly every day she expressed genuine appreciation for me. Material possessions took a backseat. After a full year of her direct and indirect appreciation, I finally realized that she did love me just for being me, not for what I did for her. Soon I was looking for every opportunity to meet her needs and our family's needs. I didn't think of denying her that furniture she wanted for years. Now that I knew her expectations weren't on the furniture, I felt free to buy it for her. We made a major project of it and spent several thousand dollars furnishing our home the way that she had always wanted.

I have met wives so content in their personal relationships with God, their husbands, and their families that they are able to live happily in circumstances as they are, with the philosophy, "What you've got is not nearly as important as who you've got."

KEEP A "HONEY-DO" LIST OF MATERIAL NEEDS

This last approach may turn many men off, but for some, like myself, it provides a handy reminder of genuine needs. A "Honey-Do" list is a record of material needs you would like your husband to meet within a given period of time. The items on the list should be reasonable and attainable for your husband with your budget. It serves as a "preview" of family needs, releasing your husband from the pressure of unexpected expenses. Use your sensitivity to determine whether your husband would genuinely appreciate a list like this. If you sense he is interested, begin to work on the list *together* and put the items in order according to their importance. If you notice your husband feeling burdened with the list, by all means revise it or tear it up. Its purpose is to ease, not increase his load.

I'm for all husbands meeting their wives' material needs in a loving way. I'm confident that you can motivate your husband to do this by living the five approaches I described in this chapter. But I hope you will keep your affection and desire centered upon the Lord and your husband instead of material possessions. Only *relationships* afford lifelong satisfaction.

FOR PERSONAL REFLECTION

Application of Philippians 4:6–7:
1. Make a list of your important household needs.
2. Calmly and expectantly let the Lord know about your list of needs.
3. In a spirit of thanksgiving let your husband know about your earnest prayer list. Let him know that if God directs him to help, you'll be thrilled.
4. Accept the Lord's *peace* as you *wait* for Him to answer your prayer, possibly and hopefully through your husband.

15

How To Increase And Deepen Your Husband's Affection For You

"He who sows sparingly shall also reap sparingly; and he who sows bountifully shall also reap bountifully."

2 Corinthians 9:6

Tim glanced across the breakfast table at Ruth. As he looked at her, he came to a sickening realization—"I don't feel any love for her anymore . . . why am I even married to this woman?"

Obviously, Tim's ailment couldn't be cured with two aspirin and plenty of fluids. He was suffering from the age-old problem of unrealistic expectations, thinking his mate would always be the twenty-year-old he married. But she had changed in the past eight years.

Typically, most of us expect our mates to retain their original physical and emotional attractiveness. But a funny thing happens on the way to retirement . . . we change. And if we change the things our mates once found attractive, we have to replace them with something better.

Even in the courtship phase of your relationship, his affection for you didn't "just happen." It grew in response to something he liked about you. Perhaps his feelings were stirred by your appearance, your personality, or the way you made him feel. If you have disposed of those positive qualities, his love for you may have dwindled to apathy.

During the courtship days, you probably had limited exposure to your fiancé. It was easy for each of you to put the other's needs or best interests first since you didn't have to do it twenty-four-hours a day. Obviously, if your fiancé was putting your best interests first and fulfilling your needs to the neglect of his own, your heart was melting daily in response to him, and vice versa.

After marriage, things quickly changed. The exposure was no longer limited to times when you were both "at your best." His own interests began to take precedence over yours and vice versa. Under these circumstances it didn't take long for swelling affections to subside.

That's why "the other woman" is at such an advantage. She can offer the new attractions your husband assumes you have lost. She can quickly stir the deep, romantic feelings your husband longs to feel toward you. In the context of their brief encounters, both of them can temporarily subdue their self-centered natures and put the best foot forward.

What specifically can you do to increase your inward beauty which is naturally reflected through your eyes and facial expressions and definitely increases your attractiveness?

KEEP A SPARK BURNING

There are several ways you can "keep a small spark burning" in your husband's heart for you. I know that you would love to see your husband initiate romance, but you may have to light the fire yourself for a while. Even though you begin to practice some of the following ideas, your husband may not fall head-over-heels in love with you overnight. However, his affections will change gradually. So don't be surprised if someday you wake up and he's the one kissing *you* on the cheek. Be prepared, in the meantime, for his shock, laughter, or even negative response to your romantic attempts. Just let him know that you love him and that you are trying to express your love in special ways. The ideas I suggest are by no means all-encompassing. There are probably thousands of ways to bring romance into your relationship. Hopefully mine will serve as a springboard for your own creative ways.

Plan activities that will make him feel special.

Here you can let your imagination run wild. Although the possibilities are endless, you know what type of activities would make your husband feel special. Perhaps his favorite meal by candlelight or a weekend getaway to his favorite resort. Whatever the activity, you can always enhance it by wearing his favorite perfume or a dress he really likes.

By planning special activities from time to time and adding a little variety, you will be showing him how special you think he is. He may not offer praise right away. Don't expect it. If you persist, eventually he will respond with praise and increased affection.

Occasionally be the initiator in the sexual area of your relationship.

Men usually initiate sexual advances in marriage, and do not really need preparation to be sexually aroused. A woman, on the other hand, needs to be prepared with gentle loving romance. Her responsiveness to sexual advances may even be affected by her husband's behavior over the past days and weeks. Although you understand this, your husband may not. Even though it may seem unnatural, it is important that you occasionally initiate intimacy if you wish to increase his affection for you.

If you have been belittled, crushed, criticized, or beaten down through the years, it may be extremely difficult for you to initiate sex. Many women have said that making love with their husbands without being emotionally prepared makes them feel like prostitutes. For a woman to engage freely in love-making, she has to give her whole self to her lover. When she is unable to do this because of his bad treatment or inadequate preparation, she feels as if he is simply using her body. If you have felt similarly toward your husband, it may sound nauseating to initiate sex with him on sheer will-power. However, as your relationship grows and deepens, you will find it more natural to give yourself to him and even initiate sexual intimacy.

When you do initiate it from time to time, use imagination to make the bedroom and your appearance as inviting as possible. Perfume, candlelight, gentle words, and a soft touch are just a few of the ways you can add creativity to the occasion.

Another way to make the occasion more fulfilling for you and your husband is for each of you to concentrate on meeting each other's sexual needs. I have found that a selfless, giving attitude contributes most to sexual enjoyment. A man's greatest fulfillment comes when he puts his whole heart into stimulating his wife and bringing her to a climactic experience. At the same time, a woman is most fulfilled when she concentrates on meeting her husband's needs. Selfish sex does nothing but remove the potential for maximum pleasure.

Needless to say there are dozens, if not hundreds, of books written by authorities on how to make the bedroom experience more fulfilling. But I firmly believe that sex at its best happens when a husband begins to meet his wife's emotional needs on a daily basis. All the techniques and atmosphere in the world can't warm up a neglected wife.

Remain flexible.

Most women would like to have their days scheduled from beginning to end, with no surprises. Schedules can be beneficial when they provide a guide for the day, but they can also become inflexible taskmasters. The day is ruined for some women when one item on their schedule has to be changed. All they can think about when their husbands come home is, "I'm behind on my schedule, and tomorrow will be worse if I don't catch up before bedtime."

If you want your marital relationship to deepen, it is very important that you learn to be flexible. I believe there is nothing as important to you or your family as a good, loving relationship with your husband. Your flexibility can make your husband feel really special and can keep that "spark" in your relationship. When he comes home and sees that you are willing to set aside your schedule for an unrushed conversation, he feels valued and loved.

Occasionally I come home late at night after meeting with a couple or a group. It really means a lot to me when my wife wakes up and spends a few minutes listening to me unwind as I tell her about my evening. Sure she's making a sacrifice, but it makes me feel important and deepens my affection for her.

Your schedule is important, I realize. However, you need to maintain a balance by being able to set aside your priorities from time to time to pay special attention to your husband and his needs. That's genuine love.

* * *

Keep yourself in good physical condition.

Health's most bitter enemies are lack of sleep and an improper diet. When they team up with constant stress, they can leave a woman irritable—not exactly an invitation to her husband's affection.

Believe it or not, one major answer to the problem of fatigue, listlessness, and irritability is regular vigorous exercise. One psychologist told me that exercise not only improves one's physical condition but also provides an excellent remedy for discouragement and depression.

Establish a routine of regular, vigorous exercise, whether it be jogging, bicycling, an exercise class, or working out at a health spa. (Be sure to consult your physician if you have any health problems that might be restrictive to certain types of exercise.)

INCREASE YOUR RESPONSIVENESS TO YOUR HUSBAND

A man loves a responsive woman. In fact, a man's self-confidence is directly related to the way others respond to him. A man will tie his affection to those who respond to him and remove it from those who don't. There are at least two ways you can increase your responsiveness to your husband.

Maintain an openness and willingness to yield to him.

I am not talking about the doormat concept of blind submission. God gave you a mind and feelings that He never intended your husband to trample underfoot. But I am talking about the willingness *to be open* to whatever your husband has to say. A willingness to hear him out and yield, if you can do so without violating your own conscience. This type of submission is not a sign of weakness, but a sign of genuine maturity (Eph. 5:22).

You know your child is growing up when he or she begins to notice and defer to the needs of others. Likewise, adults demonstrate maturity when they are willing to submit for the sake of one another. A man needs to have a submissive attitude toward his wife by considering her feelings and unique personality when making decisions. He needs to be willing, at times, to yield to her preferences. The more mature we are, the more willing we are to yield to one another.

In marriage, submission is not always simultaneous. Someone has to begin. If it doesn't start with your husband, then why not let it start with you. Perhaps he'll take advantage of your submission at first, but eventually he may take up your mature approach himself.

Carefully consider what your husband says without reacting to him.

Give attentive consideration to what your husband says *without* reacting negatively. Don't just accept the surface meaning of his statements. Ask questions and probe gently until you have a thorough understanding of what he's really trying to say.

Don't play mind reader. Too many wives assume they know their husbands well enough to predict what they are going to say. Some wives even claim to know their husbands' hidden motives. If you're going to assume anything, I hope that you will assume pure motives on your husband's part. If you do, you will be much less resistant and much more responsive to his statements. Don't react to his statements while he's speaking, but consider them and retain anything of value in them.

"You're just being weak," one husband said when his wife asked for an occasional "I love you." Needing reassurance of his love, verbally she had been slapped in the face. Obviously her affectionate feelings were dampened by his comment. Had she only stepped out of the circle of offense and taken time to consider his response, she could have learned a lot—that she needed to share why his expressions of love were important, that he approached the subject from a different reference point, and that he had *not* intended to hurt her.

As you become more responsive to your husband by learning to yield and not react, you will increase his self-confidence and self-worth. As a result, he'll gain a deeper affection for you.

KEEP THE IMAGINATION IN YOUR RELATIONSHIP ALIVE

Most of us are not fond of our daily ruts. We flock to the unusual, the novel, the unexpected in life. It's no wonder that routine marriages break up. There are too many interesting carnivals all around. When a wife can predict her husband's every mood and a husband can predict his wife's, their marriage is in for trouble. As they say, "Variety is the spice of life." So let's put some spice into your marriage.

I jog two to five miles every day, but I never take the same route two days in a row. I don't want my jogging to become monotonous. Variety keeps it interesting. The same holds true for your marriage relationship. Monotony can't set in when you add variety to your dinners, your conversations, your outings, your dates, your sex life, and your appearance.

One of the best ways to keep the imagination alive in your

relationship is to be well-informed. Ask your friends how they add creativity to their marriages. Read books and magazines about subjects that would stimulate interesting conversation. My wife contributes so much to the variety of our marriage because she is constantly learning. She not only keeps her mind alert by reading, but she also takes courses on nutrition, gourmet cooking, and other special subjects. It seems she always has something new and interesting to talk about.

CLEAR UP YOUR PAST OFFENSES TOWARD HIM

In chapter 7 we discussed the importance of clearing up offenses against your husband. It would probably be beneficial to review that chapter now.

Each time you offend your husband without clearing it up, you drive a wedge in your relationship. Nothing will remove that wedge except your humble request for his forgiveness. Write down at least three or four things you have done recently to offend your husband. Then go to him with a humble attitude and ask his forgiveness as we discussed in chapter 7. You might even take it a step further and ask him what other areas of your life offend him.

Sally was afraid to try this because her close friend had been blasted when she asked her husband how she could improve as a wife and mother. "But I'm still planning on doing it," Sally said, "because I saw how much it improved my friend's marriage." Sally's friend had finally let her husband's correction sink in and take effect. "She stopped dominating and let him lead out in public," Sally told me, "and it really improved their relationship."

Perhaps the greatest step toward maturity is learning how

to admit when we are wrong. When we can humbly seek another's forgiveness, we not only clear the offense but we also gain the respect of the offended one. What takes more courage—ignoring your offense or admitting it? The only time I ever sensed a negative reaction when I asked for forgiveness was when I asked with an accusing attitude. When others sensed a lack of genuine sorrow, they often reacted with bitterness or anger. But when they sensed a sincere grief on my part, their respect for me seemed to increase. Not only is God drawn to the humble—so are others (James 4:6).

REMAIN A CHALLENGE TO YOUR HUSBAND

I've discovered a deep truth in Proverbs: "If a man is hungry, almost anything is sweet; if he is full, even honey is distasteful" (Prov. 27:7, my paraphrase). What a powerful statement of human nature—we all tend to desire what we cannot have and become bored with what we have conquered.

Before you married, you probably were your husband's number one challenge. He got more of a charge out of winning you than anything else in life.

A man is often willing to set aside everything—relationships, projects, vocation—in order to pursue the woman he wants to marry. Unfortunately, soon after the wedding his sense of challenge departs, and he "buries himself" in projects, vocation, and other relationships. "Ah, but if I play hard to get, that'll get my husband's attention," you say. No, that may only frustrate him. But if you maintain a confident independence, showing him that he is not your sole purpose for living, he will feel challenged once again.

Before we were married, I dated my wife sporadically over

a period of four years. It seemed Norma was always available. I could call her on a moment's notice and she was always ready to go out with me. She was easy to talk to, and I loved being with her. But I took Norma for granted—perhaps because she was always available when I called her.

Then one day I heard she was dating another guy. For some strange reason my affection for her increased immediately. I thought I was going to lose her. I pursued her vigorously—all the way to the altar. But once we were married, the challenge was over. Boredom began to set in for both of us. Through many of the principles in this book, we overcame the boredom, and to this day Norma remains a challenge to me. I know she is not totally dependent upon me for her happiness. She has a deep relationship with God and looks to Him for her ultimate fulfillment (Ps. 62:1–2; Eph. 3:19–20).

USE YOUR NATURAL ATTRACTIVE QUALITIES

Several years ago a friend of mine was attending a retreat for college students. He had been married for about four years and was actively involved in counseling college-age young people. On the retreat, a very attractive young blonde came to him for counseling. In a moment of emotion, she put her arms around him seeking his comfort. He tells me that to this day, six years later, he can still remember her soft and gentle embrace. He said that in the course of his marriage his wife, who had been so gentle and affectionate when they were dating, had never touched him so softly. But one moment with that young girl had melted him. He said he hasn't seen her since, but he's never forgotten her soft voice and gentle touch.

What has happened to all the lovable characteristics that first attracted your husband to you? Perhaps it was your quiet, gentle voice . . . your gentle spirit . . . your ability to listen . . . your vivacious personality . . . your keen mind . . . your sense of humor . . . whatever qualities made the total person to whom he was initially attracted. Have some of them gotten lost through the years? Do you scream for his attention now? Are you too busy to listen to him? Have you lost your sense of humor?

I realize that your husband's inattentiveness through the years may have drained you of some of these qualities, may have driven you to scream or throw things, may have caused you to ignore him. But if you are to recapture his attention, you must somehow recapture and exhibit those qualities unique to you that first drew him to you. (These same qualities are very likely what might now attract him into the arms of another woman who exhibits them.)

GENTLY TEACH HIM BY SHARING YOUR FEELINGS

Your husband may think he is one of the most affectionate men ever to walk the face of the earth. If he's not, are you willing to teach him how to be? Maybe he assumes going to bed with you is all the affection you need. But you and I both know nothing could be further from the truth. When you do share your feelings, wait for the right time and the right circumstances. Present your feelings as clearly and logically as you can. If he reacts negatively to them, wait for another time. But be persistent. Try not to pressure him, but patiently and gently explain to him how you feel.

Sharing your feelings takes persistence, but it also takes

a method that really helps a man to better understand your true feelings. The most effective method I'm aware of is called "feeling word pictures."

These are feeling words related to a man's interests or past experiences.

Here are some examples:

- I feel like I'm a sixty-minute cassette tape and you play me romantically at night like I'm a ten-minute tape.
- I feel like a towel after a full day of washing dirty trucks.
- I feel like a two-hour-old McDonald's hamburger.
- I feel like a worm after catching a big fish.
- I feel like a golf ball after 18 holes for one important tournament, discarded or ignored.

FOR PERSONAL REFLECTION
List at least five ways you are enriching your husband's life and your marriage. Remember 2 Corinthians 9:6.

16

How To Become Your Husband's Best Friend

"It is not good for the man to be alone; I will make him a helper suitable for him."

Genesis 2:18

One of the most important objectives of this book is to help you become your husband's best friend. If you achieve this goal, many of the other objectives we talked about will automatically fall into place. A best friend is someone with whom you share intimately, someone with whom you love to spend time. Maybe that doesn't describe your husband's feelings for you at present—or your feelings for him. But don't give up hope. In this chapter we will discuss some additional ways you *can* become his closest companion.

SHARE COMMON EXPERIENCES TOGETHER

Within a period of three years, I interviewed more than thirty families who were very satisfied with their inner-family relationships. Theirs was not a superficial satisfaction, but a deep love and fulfillment. The families came from diverse geographical and social settings, and their economic bases ranged from very modest to very wealthy. But all of the families had two things in common, one of which was a concern for togetherness. In each case, the husband and wife tried not to schedule independent activities that would take them away from each other or from their children on a consistent basis. They also avoided activities that would not contribute to the well-being of the total family.

Careful planning was an essential key in these homes. Though a certain degree of flexibility was present for the pursuit of individual interests, each family member worked to create a mutually supportive unit. The family, it seemed, became a "person" in itself, nourishing itself and protecting its best interests. Typically, the husband and wife spent some time in joint activities, but more time in activities including their children. When one of the family members participated in an individual activity, the others made an effort to support him or her. (For example, the whole family would turn out for a Little League ball game.)

The other striking factor common to all these happy families was their love for *camping*. My wife and I had never been inclined toward campfires and army cots, but when I discovered that all thirty "ideal" families were campers, we decided to give it a try.

I borrowed a "pop-up camper" and we made plans to camp our way from Chicago to Florida. The first night on the road we arrived in Kentucky. It was a beautiful night, and I thought, *I can really see why this draws families together*. We talked around the campfire, sang songs, and roasted hot dogs. By nine o'clock we were pleasantly tired and tucked in bed. A romantic bit of lightning flashed in the distance followed by a gentle roll of thunder. Then it happened! That gentle thunder became a deafening boom that seemed to hover over our camper. Terror seized my little troop. Rain beat against our camper so hard that it forced its way in and soaked our pillows.

Norma and I were both frozen in terror when she squeaked, "Do you think the camper will blow over?"

"Not a chance," I said. *But it might blow up*, I thought to myself.

Who would consider camping after a horror story like that? We did. In fact, we've endured far worse at times. It seems some of our worst tragedies and arguments happen on camping trips. And that's precisely why we've become avid campers. So many things can go wrong that a family is *forced* to unite just to make it through the tough parts of the trip. The good side of camping enables a couple and their children to share the beautiful sights and sounds of God's creation. For years afterward, they can reflect on the tragic and happy experiences they struggled through together. The feeling of oneness lingers *long* after the camping trip is over.

Your first attempt at scheduling family activities may be difficult due to over-commitment. If your husband or family is already worn out with too many activities, they won't be exuberant over your new ideas. You may even be too tired to consider them yourself. But you can *make* time for them by learning to use the simple word "no." When you are asked to commit yourself to an activity that you know would not benefit your family in the long run, simply say no. Or tell them you need to discuss it with your husband. If necessary, let him step in and act as a shield by saying no.

Not all individual activities are nonproductive or harmful to family life. Your love for antiques and your son's love for caterpillars makes for a healthy balance. There is no reason to cut out or infringe upon all individual interests. Flexibility will allow togetherness and individuality.

However, one family member should not expect another to participate in distasteful or offensive activities. And no family member should attempt to be another's conscience. I don't believe you should force yourself to violate your own conscience just to be together as a family. (Not participating in distasteful activities is an important part of Romans 14.) Neither should you condemn those in your family for any of their activities. If a certain family function is distasteful, simply share in a gentle, noncondemning way that you would rather not participate. I have found that when a wife stands firm on her personal convictions in a nonjudgmental manner, it only adds to her family's respect for her.

ATTACK AND CONQUER TRAGEDIES AS A COUPLE NOT AS INDIVIDUALS

Lasting friendships are built in foxholes. Nothing binds two people together faster than a common struggle against the enemy. Virtually any crisis can draw you and your husband closer, whether it be a stopped-up sink or your unwed daughter's pregnancy. No one hunts for tragedy, but if it strikes at your door, you can strengthen your marriage by dealing with it as a team.

One of America's great preachers tells how a tremendous sorrow united his family. He and his wife faced the "typical" marriage problems and their teenagers were going through the "typical" years of rebellion. Their family life was pleasant but not intimate. One day, to everyone's amazement, his wife came home and announced she was pregnant. No one was unusually excited; the last thing they felt they needed was another mouth to feed and keep quiet.

Soon after the baby was born, things changed. He became

the apple of everyone's eye. His sweet, gentle spirit was apparent from the day he came home from the hospital. The children were so in love with him they argued over who would get to babysit with him. When the baby was only a year old, he became very ill and had to be rushed to the hospital. The whole family waited anxiously for the doctor's report. That sweet little boy had leukemia. For three days and nights the family waited together in a single room, watching over their baby, praying and hoping he would live. On the third day he died. Overwhelmed with grief, they went home to start a new life without him. Never again would they take one another for granted. Their mutual love and commitment would remain strong. Without a doubt, the death of their baby was the greatest tragedy any of them had ever experienced, but out of it came a tremendous love, intimacy, and appreciation for each family member.

MAKE IMPORTANT DECISIONS TOGETHER

It was the Fourth of July, and Norma and I were getting ready for a picnic when we burst into a heated argument. After a few minutes, things had only gotten worse. We could see we were going to be late for the picnic, so we postponed the argument till later.

I was fed up with our history of arguments. It seemed we couldn't stay out of a fight for a day. I asked Norma, "Would you be willing to try a new approach for a few weeks?" She agreed.

What we agreed upon that day has had a powerful impact on our marriage. It has forced us to communicate on deeper levels than I ever thought existed, helping us to gain an understanding of our individual viewpoints. It has forced us to look beneath surface opinions and discover the very root of our own thinking. When we disagree about a situation, our commitment to this principle helps us verbalize our feelings until we understand each other. Six years have passed since we made that commitment, and it continues to work far beyond our expectations. (It's been keeping us out of arguments ever since!)

On that Fourth of July *we agreed never to make final decisions on matters that affected both of us unless we both agreed.* If we don't arrive at unity before the bus gets here, we don't get on it. We've relied on this principle in all sorts of situations. Both of us assume responsibility for sharing our feelings honestly because we know we can't go anywhere until we're in agreement.

One man told me he would have saved more than thirty thousand dollars in the stock market if he had put this principle into action six months earlier. I'm always glad to find men who are willing to admit the value of their wives' counsel. After all, no one knows a man better than his "best friend."

DEVELOP A SENSE OF HUMOR

Class reunions always bring out the funny memories of former days. Here in this corner Jack is breaking up the group clustered around him with his old sophomore jokes. Over there by the punch bowl Janet is laughing uncontrollably as she's reminded of that practical joke on her first double-date. It seems we all did more laughing in our premarital days.

You probably weren't somber and sad when your husband married you. So, if you want to be his best friend now, you may need to add a little humor to your relationship. No need to buy a clown suit. Just look for ways to tickle his funny bone. Clip those comics or cartoons that strike you as funny and save them for his enjoyment during lighthearted times. Be willing to losen up and laugh heartily when he tells a good joke. There are countless ways to add humor to your marriage. Be willing to set aside the serious quest for romance at times to enjoy just having fun together as friends.

UNDERSTAND YOUR OWN PERSONALITY TRAITS AND YOUR HUSBAND'S

We didn't develop all of our personality traits. Many of them were inborn. There are four basic temperaments that affect our personalities and all of us *tend* toward one of those temperaments. According to Tim La Haye, these four personality types can be labeled the talker, the leader, the legalist, and the unmotivated. If you don't understand your personality type and the way it interacts with your husband's, you are likely to suffer unnecessary pain and misunderstanding. Each personality type has its strengths and weaknesses. When you better understand the strengths and weaknesses of your husband's personality, you can work in harmony with him to compensate for his weakness. If you don't understand his personality type, you may react to his weaknesses whenever they clash with yours.

There is so much material on the subject of personality types that to go into detail would require another complete book. However, I have attempted to give a brief description of each personality type, some of its strengths, and some of its weaknesses.

Take this simple test to determine your own personality type and your husband's type. (You each might be a combination of two types.) Check the appropriate boxes with an

The Outgoing Types (Extrovert)   The Shy Types (Introvert)

I	II	III	IV
The Talker	*The Leader*	*The Legalist*	*The Unmotivated*
☐ forward looking	☐ cold—unsympathetic	☐ gifted	☐ calm & quiet
☐ inventive	☐ determined & strong willed	☐ moody	☐ casual
☐ undisciplined	☐ insensitive & inconsiderate	☐ analytical	☐ easygoing
☐ charming	☐ independent	☐ negative	☐ idle
☐ weak-willed	☐ hostile—angry	☐ perfectionist	☐ likeable
☐ restless	☐ productive	☐ critical	☐ spectator
☐ warm	☐ cruel—sarcastic	☐ conscientious	☐ diplomatic
☐ friendly	☐ decisive	☐ rigid & legalist	☐ selfish
☐ disorganized	☐ unforgiving	☐ loyal	☐ stingy
☐ responsive	☐ self-sufficient	☐ self-centered	☐ dependable
☐ unproductive	☐ visionary	☐ aesthetic	☐ stubborn
☐ talkative	☐ domineering	☐ touchy	☐ conservative
☐ undependable	☐ optimistic	☐ idealistic	☐ self-protective
☐ enthusiastic	☐ opinionated & prejudiced	☐ revengeful	☐ practical
☐ obnoxious—loud	☐ courageous	☐ sensitive	☐ indecisive
☐ carefree	☐ proud	☐ persecution-prone	☐ reluctant leader
☐ egocentric	☐ self-confident	☐ self-sacrificing	☐ fearful
☐ compassionate	☐ crafty	☐ unsociable	☐ dry humor
☐ exaggerates	☐ leader	☐ self-disciplined	
☐ generous		☐ theoretical & impractical	
☐ fearful & insecure			

X for your husband and an O for you. The point of the test is to show that each of us has a unique personality type and that we *tend* to marry opposites (those who complement us).

Becoming best friends is not an automatic process just because you live together. You have to learn to compensate when you are confronted daily with the faults and weaknesses of your mate. Your "best friend" relationship with him will require perseverance, patience, understanding, genuine love, and the other qualities we discussed throughout this book. As you put into practice the five suggestions we discussed in this chapter, I am confident your friendship will deepen.

FOR PERSONAL REFLECTION

List the specific ways you have been a helper or completer to your husband (Gen. 2:18).
List additional ways you could help or complete his life.

Please Don't Forget

First, don't expect miracles overnight. Nearly everything of genuine worth takes time to perfect. These principles *do* work when applied over a period of time with persistence and a loving attitude.

Second, seek after the Lord with your whole heart, and you will find Him real and fulfilling (Luke 11:9; James 4:8).

Third, don't panic or give up when you fail. As you begin to apply these principles, you may "blow it" frequently. For example, you may find yourself using "you" statements instead of "I feel" statements without even thinking about it. Don't worry. It takes time to change habits. When you find yourself failing to apply a principle, make a mental note of the situation and vow to respond correctly the next time a similar situation arises. As time passes, you'll find yourself succeeding more frequently and failing less often. Don't fall into the trap of thinking that you're a failure just because you have failings. You're only a failure when you've given up all hope and effort to succeed.

May God bless you as you dedicate yourself to a more fulfilling and loving relationship. Remember, He wants it for you as much as you do (John 15:11–13).

Resources

Brandt, Henry, with Landrum, Phil. *I Want My Marriage To Be Better*. Grand Rapids, Michigan: Zondervan Publishing House, 1976.

Collins, Gary. *How To Be a People Helper*. Santa Ana, California: Vision House Publishers, 1976.

Day, Jerry. Clinical Psychologist, Tucson, Arizona: Ideas on stress management.

Dobson, James. *What Wives Wish Their Husbands Knew About Women*. Wheaton, Illinois: Tyndale House Publishers, Inc., 1975.

Drescher, John M. *Seven Things Children Need*. Scottdale, Pennsylvania: Herald Press, 1976.

Gothard, Bill. Director and lecturer, from the Institute in Basic Youth Conflicts. Oakbrook, Illinois.

Hardisty, Margaret. *Forever My Love*. Irvine, California: Harvest House Publishers, 1975.

Hendricks, Howard. *What You Need to Know About Premarital Counseling*. Waco, Texas: Family Life Cassettes, Word, Inc.

Hockman, Gloria. "A New Way for Families to Solve Problems Together." *Family Weekly*, July 16, 1978, p. 6.

Jones, Charles. *Life Is Tremendous*. Wheaton, Illinois: Tyndale House Publishers, 1968.

LaHaye, Tim and Beverly. *The Act of Marriage*. Grand Rapids, Michigan: Zondervan Publishing House, 1970.

LaHaye, Tim. *Understanding the Male Temperament*. Old Tappan, New Jersey: Fleming H. Revell Company, 1977.

Nair, Ken. *Discovering the Mind of a Woman*. Laredo, Texas: Fiesta Publishing Co., 1982.

Osborne, Cecil G. *The Art of Understanding Your Mate*. Grand Rapids, Michigan: Zondervan Publishing House, 1970.

Wheat, Ed. Family Physician, Springdale, Arkansas: Tapes on sex in marriage: "Sex Technique and Sex Problems in Marriage," and "Love-Life for Every Married Couple."

Resources By Gary Smalley

The Blessing, co-authored with Dr. John Trent. Nashville, Tennessee: Thomas Nelson Publishers, 1986.

Many people spend a lifetime searching for their parents' love and acceptance—their "blessing." *The Blessing* looks at the powerful Old Testament concept of "blessing children" as a tool to help our *children* in the present and to help *us* deal with emotional hurts of the past.

For Better or for Best. Grand Rapids Michigan: Zondervan Publishing House, 1979, Revised Edition, 1987.
This book is written just for the wife. Discover practical ways a wife can help to strengthen her marriage and all her important relationships.

The Gift of Honor, co-authored with Dr. John Trent. Nashville, Tennessee: Thomas Nelson Publishers, 1987.
Whether we realize it or not, the degree that we value God, others and ourselves greatly determines the success or failure of all our relationships. Learn what it means to "honor" God and our loved ones and how to avoid the incredible damage that can come from "dishonoring" them.

If Only He Knew. Grand Rapids, Michigan: Zondervan Publishing House, Revised Edition, 1987.
A valuable guide to helping a husband learn how to understand and love his wife in a meaningful way. The companion volume to *For Better or For Best.*

211

FOR BETTER

Joy That Lasts. Grand Rapids, Michigan: Zondervan Publishing House, 1986.
A personal glimpse into Gary's life as he shares insights from his experience and from the Scriptures—insights that you can use to overcome worry, fear, hurt feelings, anger and other negative emotions and replace them with love, peace, and joy.

The Key to Your Child's Heart. Waco, Texas: Word Books, 1984.
Practical parenting methods, which have been featured on Dr. Jim Dobson's radio program, "Focus on the Family," including "opening your child's spirit," family contracting, and becoming a close-knit family.

The "Love is a Decision" Film series. Grand Rapids, Michigan: Zondervan Corporation.
A six-part film series where Gary goes through six principles on developing loving and lasting relationships. Your church or study group can order the film series through your local Christian film distributor or by calling Zondervan at 1-800-233-3480.

For additional information about Gary's books, his national speaking schedule, or to order the audio-cassette tapes of his "Love Is a Decision" film series, please write:

Today's Family
P.O. Box 22111
Phoenix, Arizona 85028